Gardening Classes *in*
Waldorf Schools

Gardening Classes *in* Waldorf Schools

Birte Kaufmann

Floris Books

Translated by Matthew Barton

First published in German by Verlag Freies Geistesleben, Stuttgart, Germany under the title *Der Gartenbau-Unterricht an der Waldorfschule.*
First published in English in 2015 by Floris Books

Photographs: Othmar Berndt, Birte Kaufmann and Michael Steffens

British Library CIP Data available
ISBN 978-178250-214-2
Printed in Poland

Contents

Foreword

Gardening as a school subject has great future potential. In most subjects the aim is to impart specialist knowledge of some kind, but gardening lessons are not primarily geared to teaching horticultural expertise. What is it, then, that makes the subject so valuable for children's education and development? What skills or capacities will they need in life? Will accumulating specialist knowledge help them in their later career? It seems to me that in an increasingly technological society, governed by norms, rules, rationality and uniformity, it is important that we do not lose sight of the need to nurture individuality, creativity and diversity.

The diversity and ever-changing nature of work required in the living realm of a garden offers inexhaustible opportunities for pupils to practise vital basic skills: a sense of responsibility, independence, courage, willpower, persistence, respect for the natural world and social skills are just some of the qualities closely associated with gardening work. These imponderable qualities associated with gardening in a school setting go far beyond merely factual, practical engagement with environmental concerns or questions of natural equilibrium, though these too of course are very important. Many children today lack the opportunity to explore and discover the natural world through play; and the school garden can at least offer some scope for sensory experience. What is more, gardening involves such a wide range of activities and tasks that each child can find something to excel in.

Gardening in schools thrives in the hands of idealistic people who really feel a connection with this work and get on with it without waiting to be told what to do. But as well as commitment and initiative, specialist expertise is also needed. If this work with children is to bear fruit in the long term, we have to develop insight into the pedagogical needs of every age group and recognise how best to carry out different activities and tasks. With well-trained teachers who possess a sure fund of knowledge, gardening as a school subject will be able to develop its innovative character and provide children with something very important as they develop and grow.

Little has been written about teaching gardening in schools. As a new teacher in this field I had to search far and wide to find the information I needed to develop the range of my lessons and the whole curriculum. In this book I hope I can help younger colleagues find their way into this work more easily. Offering a clear, comprehensible and practice-oriented introduction, it deals with the most important aspects and foundations of teaching this subject in schools.

Besides suggesting *how* we can shape and organise this work in certain ways, the book also examines *why* it is important to do so, yet leaving scope for each teacher to develop his or her individual ideas and approaches. This reflects one of the really valuable aspects of gardening with children, which is the sense it gives them of nature's living diversity and each garden as an individual creation. Practical examples offered here of approaches to gardening and areas to cover in lessons can only be general ideas which each school, with its own distinct locality and staff, can of course adapt as it sees fit.

In my view, gardening in schools still has a long way to go to fulfil its potential as a life-affirming subject that strengthens children's will and engagement with nature's realities, wonderfully complementing more abstract cognitive skills focused all too often only on exam results.

CHAPTER ONE

A History of School Gardens

Gardens have been important to humankind for many millennia, and they have also long been used to teach and train people. In the Middle Ages, monastery gardens were used primarily to instruct cloister novices, and sometimes lay people too, in horticulture. A little later, in 1632, Johann Amos Comenius urged schools to have a garden although this chiefly served pupils' recreation and was not yet intended to teach them about gardening.[1]

In the first half of the eighteenth century in Germany the first school gardens were established with a pedagogical intent, initially for religious and moral instruction. The very first such school garden was probably the one established by August Hermann Francke in Saxony, while the educator Julius Hecker started Berlin's first school garden in 1750.

In the last quarter of the nineteenth century, due to huge demand for plant material for teaching biology and 'object lessons' in high schools, central plant breeding and supply gardens developed in many German cities, though these were not used for pedagogical purposes.

At the end of the nineteenth century and beginning of the twentieth, school kitchen gardens were established in many countries including Britain and the United States. At this time physical activity was thought to nurture children's learning and development by inculcating virtues such as persistence, tidiness and punctuality; and direct observation of and involvement with the garden was also considered to aid and consolidate their understanding of the laws of nature. By the beginning of the 1930s, there were over 1100 school gardens across Germany.

During the Nazi era, school gardens at primary and secondary level were intended to give pupils skills that would later enable them to manage their own vegetable plots in order to support the general economy and ensure the population could feed itself in war and at times of crisis.

After the Second World War, the school garden movement that had started in the pre-war period survived to some extent into the sixties, but without any renewed impulse. It therefore gradually waned and school gardens closed. As a subject it disappeared from the curriculum.

In the GDR (East Germany), by contrast, almost all schools had gardens where children worked and learned horticulture. This work primarily served the aims of socialist education, with a focus on high yield.

The situation in Waldorf/Rudolf Steiner schools is somewhat different. While Steiner did not directly include gardening in the original curriculum, it was introduced as a regular school subject at the first Waldorf School in Stuttgart a little later, in the spring of 1920, after the available grounds had been prepared by groups of pupils.[2]

In a teachers' faculty meeting on March 6, 1920, Steiner said the following: 'but it is a different situation in the gardening class. That needs someone who really understands the subject.' This shows that he thought it very important for gardening teachers to feel a strong connection with the task and to have the necessary skills and knowledge. In his view the teacher who had been working on the school grounds with pupils until then did not have the right abilities:

> What I have seen indicated that he does not have
> sufficient practical talent so that the children could not
> do their work well because he himself does not have an
> eye for what the craft demanded ... The worst thing was
> that he simply had no heart for his work.[3]

We can already see here what might be needed to sustain the teaching of gardening:

> This will not be a matter of giving the children some
> kind of pre-career training but rather, in relation to the
> whole of the rest of the curriculum, of nurturing the
> right mood for children to appreciate the natural context
> of agriculture. This will be necessary to counter future
> catastrophes related to soil depletion ... It is of very great
> importance for social development that people feel, right
> down to their finger-tips, that they are always dependent
> on the work of others.[4]

In contrast with the school garden movement of previous decades, we here find a new pedagogical rationale and approach to the subject. Although Steiner never added any precise suggestions for gardening to the curriculum, beyond isolated statements at meetings and in lectures, gardening itself became firmly established from the beginning and is now taught at most Waldorf Schools over several years. The statements and observations by Steiner on gardening have been compiled and, along with subsequent practical experiences in this field, form the basis for the Steiner/Waldorf gardening curriculum.[5]

Many Waldorf Schools possess a smaller or larger school garden where practical gardening instruction and activities take place, and where children can have direct, hands-on experience of the natural world. The focus of these activities falls largely in middle school (Classes 6–8, age 11–14), though it often returns in a different form in Classes 9 and 10 (age 15–16).

Yet even in Waldorf Schools we can sense something of the fluctuating fortunes of school gardens. It often remains a somewhat marginal subject, and this is confirmed every year at the international gardening teachers' conference. In this group, though, continual and lively efforts are made to nurture and develop school gardening work.

Looking at the situation at present, we find many new initiatives. As well as project-type, seasonal work on small plots in schools, initiated by a few committed teachers, one also finds long-standing and regularly used school gardens of all shapes, sizes, kinds and uses. There is great diversity in the way this subject is taught, depending on the emphasis and number of lessons allocated to it in the curriculum. Sometimes gardening in lower school (Classes 2 and 3, age 8–9) takes the form of short-term project work, rather than ongoing involvement throughout the year with a wealth of changing sensory experiences of the natural world.

CHAPTER TWO

The Experience of the Natural World

Many children grow up in an urban environment without much connection to the natural world. Often they cannot just walk out of their front door and find natural environments where they move and play freely and make all kinds of discoveries. In many areas children are not even allowed out on their own since the traffic is too dangerous or because there just isn't any recreation space nearby for them to play in. And not all children have the chance to go on outings with their family to rural areas, to visit friends or relatives there, or spend holidays on farms. More and more children – not only those in big cities – are deprived of the chance to grow up in close proximity with plants and animals, and relate to the natural world.

Since it is increasingly difficult nowadays for parents to spend quality time with their children, the latter tend to spend much of their free time in front of a TV or computer. Many therefore never learn to develop their own creative ideas through play, either on their own or with their peers. It has become rare for neighbourhood children to meet together outside as they always used to do and make up games with whatever they find in the way of natural materials.

Even children who grow up in rural areas are deprived of direct contact with nature and especially with agriculture. Villages consist increasingly of houses with small gardens for commuting city workers. As farmers leave the land, rural children have fewer opportunities to witness a proper farm at work, where they could see how farm animals are raised and kept, or how vegetables are cultivated and harvested. Few farms today allow children from the neighbourhood to help or watch, or simply play in a hay barn.

Whether in rural or urban settings, many children follow a strict timetable even in their free time, with parents organising all kinds of activities for them – sport, music lessons, extra coaching, ballet etc. At school more and more children complain that they have no time to meet up with their friends or go to a birthday party since their whole week is 'booked up'.

All these things mean, firstly, that they lose an opportunity to play freely with children of their age, creatively structuring their leisure time and developing ideas from what they find around them in nature. This in turn, through lack of unforced practice and natural skill development, has a negative impact on many important motor skills such as balance and movement.

Secondly children scarcely know any more how potatoes or tomatoes actually grow. They cannot name indigenous trees, and they often think that strawberries, say, grow all year round. This lack of knowledge affects their capacity to perceive and value nature. How can a child develop respect for something that remains completely abstract? Wittkowske writes:

> Only when children are really in touch with nature will they love and protect it too. There is no doubt that development of this positive stance depends on children having an opportunity to encounter nature fully from an early age, and on their continuing to have these experiences as they grow.[1]

CHAPTER THREE

Why Teach Gardening in Schools?

In recent years, environmental education has grown hugely in importance and led to countless initiatives, projects and services in this field. One of the reasons for this is that children today need new and different means to engage with nature and have experiences of the natural world.

There is often more provision for such learning outside of schools than in them: a wide range of opportunities and facilities for children and classes at environmental and nature protection centres, including local projects and campaigns, with related teaching materials. Agricultural cooperatives collaborate with some schools and may hold community harvest days. In recent decades, farm and forest schools and Waldorf kindergartens with an emphasis on directly experiencing nature have opened.

As we saw, gardens for training and observation purposes have long existed, but their aims were very diverse, dictated by certain cultural and historical imperatives. Despite most children being unlikely to make a career of gardening, why are schools showing a renewed interest in gardening? And why has this subject been a successful part of the Waldorf curriculum for many decades, especially as a mainstay of the middle years (ages 11–14)?

This seems to be due to the fact that gardening work develops positive capacities in young people far beyond familiarity with basic gardening knowledge, and in our time, when direct experience of nature is on the wane, this acquires ever greater importance. Wittkowske summarised it: 'To perceive our surroundings is the foundation of our capacity to learn. Sensory experience of nature cultivates wonder, one of the key qualities in developing empathy.'[1]

In fact, this observation encompasses only a small portion of the complex mix of physical, psychological and intellectual benefits children can gain through garden work. Its rich variety cultivates many other capacities alongside the honing of sensory perceptions: gross and fine motor skills developed in every sequence of work, as well as the exertion and persistence required to complete tasks. In other words, children are challenged to go a little beyond their comfort zone, especially at moments when the work isn't immediately enjoyable, seems boring, demands exertion or the overcoming of squeamishness. Every form of garden work also elicits a sense of responsibility. Helmut Birkenbeil writes very aptly that 'it offers many opportunities to develop the key competency of "responsibility" in regard to oneself and others, in a context in which plants and animals also count as fellow creatures.'[2]

It must by now be obvious that development of such capacities takes time and ongoing effort. One-off projects or those severely curtailed in duration at out-of-school learning centres will certainly help to awaken the children's interest in the natural world and environmental problems, but regular, long-term work in a school garden, with its recurring activities and sequences, asks pupils to keep practising a whole host of basic skills and abilities. This goes far beyond developing 'ecological awareness' to the cultivation of all kinds of capacities children will need later in life. Birkenbeil continues:

> The prerequisites for successful gardening, such as precise observation and attentiveness, careful work, considered intervention, respect and humility for the living world, are skills transferable to other fields of life and education.[3]

Seen from another perspective, there is a very distinctive and positive aspect of school gardening, different in kind from other school subjects:

> A miniature of this kind (the school garden) offers a portion of real life, and, in a highly compressed way, is a complete, tangible biosphere. At the same time its dimensions are comprehensible.[4]

This picks up on the now widely acknowledged view that children learn better if the subjects taught have tangible reality for them. In this context Rudolf Steiner states:

> ... [tell] the children about the links between agriculture and the way humans live ... This will give them skills and will prepare them for taking their places properly in life later on ... For more important than dexterity is the soul contact made between the life of the child and the life of the world.[5]

The school garden can be a very distinctive place of learning, with a wide range of learning and developmental opportunities. In what follows we will explore some of these opportunities and reflect on the best way to make this subject a successful part of the school curriculum.

CHAPTER FOUR

Gardening and Adolescent Development

So far we have looked at why gardening is so valuable for cultivating many capacities and for children's development in general. In Waldorf Schools, gardening lessons intentionally start at a specific stage, in middle school. A few schools begin earlier with regular gardening and farming sessions, distinct from the farming main–lesson in Class 3 (age 8–9); but a study of the psychological and mental development of middle school pupils can soon show us why Steiner thought this was a good age to engage with gardening. This is clearly formulated by Tobias Richter in the Waldorf School curriculum:

> Lessons in gardening begin as puberty commences ... At this age young people need security and help in orienting themselves, and an active engagement with outdoor work is of special importance and pedagogical help here. The teacher in this subject becomes an expert who illumines and mediates natural processes and contexts.[1]

And elsewhere the same author writes: 'Gardening lessons give adolescents the opportunity to gain real understanding of the natural world.[2]'

Only at middle-school age have children developed to the point where they can really have a more conscious relationship with nature. Before this, they still have a very intimate and deeply connected sense of their surroundings: 'At kindergarten age, and often up to the age of nine or ten, children perceive the surrounding world as ensouled and animated.'[3] For this reason they are not yet able to step back from this connection and intervene in natural contexts through intentional, directed work. And only in early adolescence do they develop the physical strength to really engage in gardening. This does not mean that younger children should not garden on a smaller scale – the experience of nature they gain through this is of course very valuable; but before middle-school age this is best done more playfully, with an emphasis on nature's beauty and enjoyment of it.

The middle-school years involve great developmental strides, and each phase of this period should be studied closely to see how we can respond to it with changing pedagogical approaches. Just as the lesson content develops year by year in other subjects, gardening too must be taught in an age-appropriate way. A Class 5 (age 10–11) will need a different kind of lesson and teaching approach from a Class 8 (age 13–14). In fact, the wonderful thing about gardening is that it offers such a wealth of possibilities that we can certainly tailor it to the needs of different ages. Below we will take a look at child development through the whole span of the middle-school years and see how gardening lessons can draw on this clear foundation.

4.1 Class 5

At this stage (age 10–11) the class-teacher has reached the half-way mark of his or her eight years with a class (age 7–14). This age is marked by a certain degree of physical and psychological harmony. Having previously 'crossed the Rubicon'* around the age of nine, they have developed a new, different relationship to their surroundings and to other people, experiencing a more conscious separation between themselves and the world. As yet, though, puberty with all its turmoils and transformations has not begun to impact on them. At this age their breathing-pulse ratio usually settles into a balanced 1:4, and their breathing deepens. Head, trunk and limbs interrelate harmoniously, and they move easily and often gracefully, with as yet no signs of the physical weight and growth spurts of puberty. Inwardly and in relation to their surroundings the children at this age often feel a sense of equilibrium. They are usually eager to learn, enthusiastic and inquisitive, and wish to be challenged. For the first time, perhaps, they will start asking deeper questions about why things are the way they are. The curriculum at this age adds botany as a new subject.

Some schools start gardening at this age – either at the beginning of the school year or in the spring, when the gardening season begins. It seems to me a very good idea to start gardening lessons in the spring of Class 5, even though Steiner, in his day, suggested waiting until Class 6. First of all it makes sense to follow the cycle of the seasons and get a class engaged with gardening in the 'right' sequence of the

---

*A phrase coined by Steiner to highlight a stage in development where children emerge from a sense of unity with their surroundings and develop a somewhat more detached relationship with the world.

year's activities. And secondly we can draw on the energy, curiosity and openness to new things apparent at this age. In the past few years I have found that children at the end of Class 5 are very keen to get involved in gardening, so much so that sometimes you can scarcely rein them in. They throw themselves into it and want to do everything well. As yet they don't mind getting dirty or tired, whereas this changes in subsequent years. A good, positive beginning at this age will create habits and establish rules and ways of working that sustain the subject well into adolescence.

First sowing of seeds with Class 5

One can start in Class 5 with simple gardening tasks. Unlike earlier, where gardening is done more playfully (sowing sunflower seeds in pots, growing cress on the windowsill etc.) we now embark on 'proper gardening', learning about the common tools, how to dig, and how to sow seeds, for instance. The chosen activities should satisfy the children's need to be active without physically overtaxing them, nor confusing them with over-complex sequences. It is very important for lessons to allow time for the children's sensory observations: during the first months it is good to let them simply 'discover' the garden with its range of different plants, and observe how these grow and develop.

Let them watch butterflies, smell herbs, sample vegetables or observe worms. The focus at this age is on experiencing the life of a garden, with its ecology and the work required there. It is not yet a matter of 'conveying knowledge' intellectually. This approach will form the basis for more precise and intense engagement with different areas of work and natural phenomena in the years to come.

4.2 Class 6

During this year we start to see the first signs of pre-puberty. Children develop a noticeably more distant relationship with the adults close to them (parents/teachers), and are no longer so forthcoming about their feelings, thoughts and experiences. In the class community we start to see little 'groups' and cliques forming, within which 'secrets' are passed around. They start to voice their criticisms clearly and question adult decisions. The girls become more aware of and concerned with their appearance. The first physical changes become apparent, and as they start to grow taller many will start to look somewhat gawky.

At this age, causal thinking becomes possible, a sense of the connection between cause and effect. Rudolf Steiner remarks:

> Before the approach of the twelfth year, the concept of causality does not exist in the minds of children ... this concept must be avoided at all costs until this time, and then we may consider a newly emerging understanding for the relationship between cause and effect. Only at that time do children begin to have their own thoughts about various things. Previously they saw the world in pictures.[4]

The curriculum responds to this new capacity by embarking on science, with precise observations and descriptions of phenomena. Increasingly in lessons the children's gaze is focused on the outer world.

Pupils are still active and interested in the school garden at this age. They get to grips with it energetically and are proud of 'their' harvest. They eagerly pull carrots, patiently search for potatoes or carefully pluck tomatoes (either at the first harvest of their own produce in the autumn

A Class 6 girl works on her plot

if they started gardening in Class 5, or at the end of Class 6 or beginning of Class 7). They now learn all basic gardening skills – digging, raking, hoeing, planting and care of beds, sowing etc.

To begin with these tasks are done together, but gradually – especially if gardening began in Class 5 – in a more differentiated fashion. Becoming acquainted with the garden and experiencing its life remains central. This year it is important for chosen tasks to be such that pupils easily see the point of them. We can discern the 'causal principle' everywhere at work in the garden! It quickly becomes apparent that careful sowing and cultivation has a direct impact on the abundance of a harvest. It is also important for pupils to recognise that garden work takes precedence over their own immediate concerns, and that their own actions therefore have consequences – not just in relation to the long-term health of the soil and plants but also as regards their own little rewards in lessons: if they complete the necessary tasks reliably, then they will have time at the end to sit together and drink a tea made from herbs they have picked, or sample the fruits they have harvested.

At this age one notices that rules are gradually questioned and tested, and so it is important to base these on a clear, comprehensible rationale. The period when the teacher was regarded as a natural authority is ending. But rules and instructions have a purpose: if they can be accepted they will sustain the class through subsequent school years as the children's desire to challenge and push boundaries increasingly comes to the fore, along with a wish to discuss and debate. Yet every pupil will immediately recognise that a garden fork, say, must be carried with the tines pointing downwards so that it doesn't injure anyone.

4.3 Class 7

During this year one can observe children turning into adolescents. Tendencies that were not yet very pronounced the year before now come to the fore more strongly: the need to argue, discuss, to put one's opinion and question everything is ongoing. Increasingly young people can make 'rational judgments' although this capacity is still

A Class 7 girl harvests flowers and herbs from her plot

greatly influenced by subjective feelings. Children's innate inwardness gives way to strong outward expression of feelings. Emotional volatility becomes very discernible and often affects young people's decisions: situations, tasks and people are judged in terms of like and dislike. Physically, young people are growing taller, and external sexual characteristics are developing.

The Waldorf curriculum responds to this by further developing and deepening science lessons, practising clear causal thinking and objective judgment.

In gardening lessons, changes in the pupils' behaviour and work become noticeable: the enthusiasm and commitment of previous years increasingly gives way to a view that almost all gardening work is too tiring and too much to expect of them. Whenever tasks are allocated, there will be much argument, discussion and 'negotiation': 'Can't someone else do that job? Do we really have to do this today? Wouldn't it be OK just to do half the amount of work and get a different group to do the rest?' If these arguments remain fruitless, discussion moves to the 'next level': 'I already did that – so-and-so never has!' or, 'If we do it quickly, can we still eat something together or end the lesson early?' This argumentativeness is on the one hand a genuine desire to clarify

things, but it also often has an underlying intent: to waste as much time as possible so that less work is done.

Tasks in the gardening lesson are now accomplished with less care and precision. The pupils' main aim is to get 'disagreeable work' over quickly. Seed drills, for instance, are marked 'by eye' only, with poor regard for sowing depths and less care for the spacing of seeds. If the teacher is not alert, prunings are tipped anywhere instead of the place where they're meant to be collected, or, instead of weeding properly, earth is merely spread about the place in the hope that no one will notice. Tools are often no longer cleaned properly or put back in their right places. At the same time the young people easily get distracted or diverted from the task in hand, and prefer chatting to each other.

It is important for a teacher not to take this personally but to recognise this new, somewhat tiring behaviour for what it is: a necessary phase of development. Adolescents will benefit if the teacher remains calm, and shows a good deal of 'stubborn' persistence, clarity and honesty. Only in this way can they learn to handle boundaries and accept them. Humour is vital for handling such situations. This makes it much easier for the pupils to respond to and engage with the tasks that are set, and helps them more easily develop a new relationship with the teacher, founded on acceptance.

Consistency, persistence and above all care and precision should be accentuated and demanded in gardening this year. Precise, clear tasks, with clearly determined aims offer a constant reminder that *how* one does a job is important. The garden itself is a great help here, for in a sense it is the 'teacher'. Since every action in the garden has direct, visible consequences, gardening demands of pupils, in a benevolent, authentic way, exactly what they need at this age: a real confrontation with the effects of their own actions in relation to the natural world.

4.4 Class 8

Now the young people are in the midst of puberty and, in developmental terms, on their way to achieving 'earthly maturity'. This phase gives adolescents the sense, often, that they are very much alone, facing new, unknown situations, and struggling to find their own place in the world. The feeling of loneliness can be marked, leading many pupils to withdraw and cut themselves off at this time. The time when teachers were seen as authority figures has certainly passed now. But by showing their expertise and professionalism, as well as a humorous, respectful and calm demeanour, they can regain adolescents' respect.

The curriculum responds to this stage of development with themes and tasks that draw the pupils' concerns away from themselves and their own vulnerabilities towards a newly awakening interest in the world. For instance, the biographies of well-known figures can show them that each person can meet and surmount difficulties in life, and do so in a very individual way. In other words they discover that in terms of their own inner struggles they are not alone in the world. The individual project which each pupil undertakes this year requires intensive, individual and self-motivated involvement with a self-chosen topic, as a kind of model of how each adolescent can find 'their own way'. By contrast the class play at the end of Class 8 requires them to relate their own ideas, wishes and ways of behaving to other realities by entering into a different role or character.

At the beginning of Class 8, in gardening lessons, we can start to sense pupils' unexpressed desire to be addressed differently and more like adults, to be taken more seriously, even if their own behaviour does not always elicit this. They make it clear that repetitive gardening activities they are familiar with from past years are no longer enough to keep them

interested and motivated. New tasks are therefore needed to do justice to this age. More autonomy and responsibility, the opportunity for them to have more say in what happens, can now form the basis for gardening lessons. Theoretical aspects of gardening (such as crop rotation or different soil types) can also complement activities. In schools where no new emphases emerge but instead the same old activities are simply repeated, the subject often suddenly falls out of favour, possibly leading to reluctance to follow instructions, or even severe disruption of lessons.

In gardening for this year it is a good idea to give more individual tasks that relate as far as possible to each pupil's particular interests. Areas of work become more complex and demanding, both physically and intellectually, and should require their full attention: these can include building projects, the processing of harvested produce, and the manufacture of ointments and tinctures, with an increased emphasis on self-reliance, precision and careful planning. It is helpful to divide the group into small teams to ensure that individuals start to take more responsibility.

4.5 Class 9: Work experience on a farm

Marking the entry into upper school, Class 9 represents a new stage in young people's schooling, informed by awakening awareness and accompanied by all sorts of questions about life, about their own relationship with the earth, with other people, with animals and plants. They cast a critical eye on such matters, and question social conditions and structures as well as industrial and technical 'achievements' in the modern world.

Towards the end of Class 8, lessons in the school garden come to an end, and now, with work experience on a farm, the view broadens to encompass larger contexts and real relationships between work, ways of living, food production and natural processes in which we are

Cooking as individual and teamwork

either more or less directly involved. In the form of practical work and the experiences gained through it, work experience on a farm enables young people to formulate direct questions about important aspects of life, and to ask critical questions. Topics here include the relationship between the work needed to create food and the 'value' this is accorded in terms of wages, or the quality of food related to agricultural practice (organic versus conventional agriculture). How animals are reared, kept, and slaughtered to produce meat, also becomes a pressing concern.

These questions are the first foundation for considering broader social issues, and the slow emergence of each individual's personal stance towards them through the upper school years.

The farming work experience at Waldorf Schools in Germany (it varies in other countries) chiefly happens in one of two forms. For two to four weeks either the whole class goes to a larger farm together, or pupils are sent alone or in twos to a farm. If you ask schools about their experiences with these, you will find proponents and opponents of both forms, since each has advantages and disadvantages.

If the farming experience involves a whole class on a farm, this can have a very striking effect on the class community. It is often at this point that old, habitual social forms in the class break down, giving rise to new configurations and friendships. In this intensive period of practical work, class members perceive their classmates in a quite different way from daily school life, and this usually has very positive outcomes. The new class guardians who almost always accompany the class on this work experience, also have the chance here to develop a relationship with the class and get to know individual pupils better.

If a whole class is to stay on a farm together, the farm itself must be prepared for this and able to cope with it, not only having sufficient accommodation but also, above all, a wide enough range of well-supervised work activities. Pupils are usually divided into smaller groups that work at various places on the farm, and change activity at intervals so that by the end of the work experience all have engaged with every sphere of work (for instance stable work and animal care, vegetable cultivation, baking, dairy and cheese-making,

Three satisfied pupils during work experience

'Afternoon nap' during a tour of one of the farms prior to work experience

maintenance, forestry work, and so on). On many farms this daily work is supplemented by lessons in farming principles and theory, in which the farmer, farm workers or apprentices give the pupils deeper insight into aspects of agriculture.

In this form of the practical there is a danger, however, that age-related social dynamics in the class can negatively impact on some pupils' attitude to work and commitment. In other words, it is sometimes hard for some teenagers to get to grips with the new situation and engage with it fully in front of friends who are used to their behaving in a certain way, especially if the work is associated with making an effort, getting dirty or with unpleasant smells. It is therefore very important to supervise what happens with alertness and expertise, so that pupils gain a sense that every helping hand is needed. If a class is only given 'simple tasks' without much variety, such as endless hedge trimming, they will feel exploited, superfluous or not fully appreciated. They will quickly lose interest and fail to engage, making the work experience a 'hard slog' in the wrong sense, which in retrospect has led neither to a serious and critical involvement with this kind of work nor with the broader life questions it raises. Apart from this, groups of this age are likely to be trying out alcohol, cigarettes or drugs, which can mean that those supervising the work experience have to keep an eye on pupils in their free time as well.

If the young people are sent alone or in pairs to a farm, the pedagogical emphasis lies elsewhere. It can often be seen as positive that pupils spend a while away from the class community and can therefore get away from their 'habitual roles' within it, giving them a free space to develop. At the same time of course it requires more courage to engage with a new situation without the protection and familiarity of the group. The emphasis is likely to be much more on self-reliance and independence, since pupils will probably make the first contact with the farm alone, and also travel there independently. During work experience the young people will be much more dependent on their own resources than they would be in the group. They will have to form closer contact with people on the farm and be more fully involved in their lives and work. This is a schooling in capacities of great importance today: courage, initiative, self-reliance, commitment and persistence. In this form of the work experience it has been found that most young people, despite their worries and disinclination beforehand, really do get very involved and quickly identify with the work and 'their farm'. For a long time afterwards they continue to speak of their experiences there, and sometimes will return to visit or help with harvest.

Alongside the positive aspects of this form of farm experience, 'allocating' the pupils to many different farms involves a lot of organisation as well as preparatory work with parents and the class, and the forging of close links with the farms themselves. It also requires clear rules and agreements with all involved to ensure the practical time runs smoothly and is a positive experience all round. If preparation and planning is not sufficiently differentiated and transparent, this can quickly lead to dissatisfaction on the part of parents, pupils and the farms, which will also make it harder to organise work experience in future years. There will only be a limited number of suitable or available farms willing to undertake this. If their experience is one of difficulties with the pupils or their parents, they will eventually stop participating. Increasingly schools do adopt this form of the work experience, but there are not necessarily enough farms to go round.

4.6 Class 10: Plant selection and grafting

At this age young people have more or less finished going through puberty, and their own personality is developing more clearly. The focus of the learning process now is to acquire clear thinking and, through further practice of causal relationships in all domains, to develop an ability to make objective, logical and rational judgments. Increasingly they become aware of how their own actions affect the world and others around them: they start to take responsibility for themselves and become conscious citizens of the earth.

Gardening this year is concerned with plant selection and grafting, as it were the crowning conclusion of this subject. Intentional human intervention in the plant world – usually illustrated in relation to the apple tree – highlights the responsibility each person bears towards living things. Since human beings first began to cultivate nature and make use of it for their own purposes, the breeding and selection of wild plants to create crops (grains, fruits etc.) has placed us in a responsible role. These cultivated plants, with their specific modifications to make them of use to us, could not go on existing in the natural world without constant care and attention. Engagement with this theme at this age can be extremely valuable since there are very tangible connections here with incipient developmental progress in the young people themselves: to keep on developing through a lifetime, people must make decisions about how they wish to be, actively guiding the process of their own development and taking responsibility for their actions.

The theme of grafting is usually dealt with in a lesson block rather than over the whole school year. Following a theoretical introduction and preparatory practicals, the block ends with all pupils grafting their 'own' apple tree which, in some schools continues, to be cultivated in the school garden through to the time of the school-leaving exams, and is then given to the pupils in a concluding festival and celebration. Unfortunately, though, this is only done at a few Waldorf Schools nowadays. The time pressures in the upper school, and the wide range of subjects needing to be covered often mean that this lesson block is sacrificed. There may also often be a lack of teachers with the right expertise. And yet closer study can show that there are very few subjects which illustrate in such a vivid way real parallels with the young people's developmental stage, and therefore offer such a fine opportunity to engage with ideas about the importance of responsible human action.

Project work by a Class 8 group: revamping of old chairs for the gardening room

CHAPTER FIVE

Various Teaching Methods

In many schools, much emphasis is placed on the social aspect in gardening lessons in the middle school. Developmentally, a prime task at this age is to direct child's gaze 'out into the world' and away from their own inner state; the 'tumult of feelings' that often dominates this phase. Science lessons begin and require, for the first time, a capacity to observe objectively and descriptively, without lapsing into subjective, feeling-coloured judgments. This 'widening of horizons' extends also to study of the destinies of other people and nations and to social concerns on a smaller or larger scale.

Thus the school garden is often seen as the 'common property' of the school community, and run with the aim of showing that the classes working in it are doing so for all, and not for themselves.

But we need to ask how gardening tasks can be shaped in a sufficiently differentiated way that takes account of different ages and their specific needs, so that children can perceive purpose in what they are doing and develop enjoyment and interest in it. Especially in the later phase of middle school, as puberty kicks in, the pupils themselves demand this. If this does not happen, the lessons can soon degenerate.

The school garden offers a great diversity and range of work. It is therefore worth looking very carefully in advance at which tasks are suitable for which groups and which individual pupils. There are wonderful opportunities for differentiation here: according to age, the group's ability to concentrate and work together, or in catering for specific individuals. Ultimately too we must be aware of our own skills and limitations. Depending on the situation it can be useful to choose between group, team or individual tasks and look very carefully at which is the most suitable approach.

Differentiation and individualisation in teaching have assumed increasing importance in recent years in all subjects and forms of schooling since classes increasingly consist of children with very diverse abilities and learning needs. Gardening work offers excellent opportunities for attending to the strengths, weaknesses and needs of individual pupils and, in certain situations, for creating an individual support programme.

5.1 Working in a group

Sometimes working in the group is thought to be an especially desirable aspect of the gardening lesson. Here the prime focus, corresponding with developmental themes of middle school, is on practising social capacity and looking beyond one's own immediate interests. But here too we must bring a differentiated approach to bear: working together in large groups *can* be very useful and helpful in certain situations and for particular types of work, but equally can mean that individual children rely too much on the work of their fellow pupils and do not get as fully involved as they should. Especially at middle-school age, individual responsibility can quickly become submerged in the group as a whole, giving a sense that one's own work is of little overall importance. When weeding or sowing, for instance, it is often hard to see who has done what where, and therefore whose work was better or worse. It may also be that in whole-group work some children are over-taxed while not enough is asked of others.

This does not mean that working in a group is not a good idea. There are certainly jobs where this is advantageous, especially in situations where large quantities have to be moved such as transporting and cutting up wood after a tree has been cut down, trimming a long hedge, working on large compost sites, digging over a large bed, raking leaves, harvesting fruit etc. Together in a group the children can experience the value of numbers, accomplishing tasks that would have been too much for them alone.

In shared undertakings of this kind it is important to assign children to specific areas and sections of the work: to decide who is shovelling, who pushing the wheelbarrow, who is sawing, who is piling up logs etc. Without this there is a danger that things get chaotic, that children mainly just do the things they enjoy, or join in where their friends are working. We should always try to impart a sense that a successful outcome depends on each individual pulling their weight. It is especially rewarding when pupils themselves notice where the process is running smoothly or faltering, and start to urge each other on or point out what needs doing.

Work in a large group is particularly suited to the beginning of gardening lessons in Class 5 and 6. At this age children are usually still eager and involved, and like making an effort. Apart from this, their physical size at this age means they get more done together. They can take great pleasure in what they have accomplished as a group.

5.2 Individual jobs and small teams

From around Class 7 it becomes apparent that pupils are starting to question what they do: Why do I have to do this? Do we really have to do it? Can't someone else do it? Suddenly every spade stroke seems endlessly tiring and quickly leads to indignant complaints about these 'unreasonable' demands.

Pupils start to take less care with their work, rushing through jobs they don't enjoy. It is therefore worth taking time now and then to check a bed that has supposedly been dug over and weeded. Quite often you'll find the weeds still just below the surface, left there in the hope that the teacher will not notice.

Harvesting beans together on the Class 6 beds

Two pupils prepare a class bed together

At this age it is a good idea to allocate more individual jobs and work in small teams. The advantage of this is that individual pupils cannot duck out of things by 'hiding' in the group. One can see exactly what each individual has done (or not) and challenge those whose work falls short. With small teams one can also counter the cliques and dynamics that develop at this age, separating certain pupils (whether friends or 'troublemakers').

Since pupils by now have usually been having gardening lessons for a while, they are familiar with the garden, the jobs and the tools. This is important when working in small groups or teams, which stretches the supervision capacities of the teacher. Well-differentiated preparation and planning must be done ahead of the lesson, with consideration given to individual pupils' abilities, and the complexity of tasks to be accomplished.

5.3 Projects

By 'projects' I mean lessons or jobs that are undertaken independently of seasonal work and horticultural 'necessities', and last only a limited time. These can of course form part of normal gardening lessons,

Some jobs are best done alone, and require special skill and accuracy

though perhaps with some extra time added if need be: a building project in the garden (for instance a cold frame, a spiral bed for herbs, an insect hotel or suchlike), or the organising of a plant sale or garden festival. One can of course also run projects outside of normal gardening lessons, undertaken for example with the class teacher or parents. Or individual pupils can be given the opportunity to choose specific jobs and get more deeply involved in them.

Project-oriented work is becoming increasingly important in many schools, and for many subjects represents a very useful form of learning support. This approach only figures to a limited extent in gardening, which is devoted primarily to an experience of the seasons and associated work. In other words, the garden more or less dictates what we need to do at any point in the year, and renders 'devised' projects superfluous. Apart from this, gardening lessons are a counterbalance to the speedy nature of modern culture and the search for quick rewards: they require persistence and perseverance, and these qualities can therefore intentionally be accentuated as puberty begins.

But as already mentioned, there are situations where project work can usefully enhance and complement other gardening jobs. Building projects can be very valuable but one has to be clear how they can be practically realised. It is usually a good idea to collaborate with other

Several classes work together to beautify a cold frame in the school garden

colleagues in cross-curricular fashion, or undertake them with the help of parents, planning in extra time to do so: project weeks, action days etc. We have to make sure that a project like this does not get in the way of regular gardening work but that the latter continues alongside.

Of course there are also circumstances where a school does not have the facilities to offer gardening all through the year and yet would still like to have a school garden. In such cases smaller or bigger projects of limited duration can be undertaken. For instance, a class or group could cultivate just one type of crop, planting a potato field, say, or work with various herbs and their processing to make herb salts, teas and ointments.

Some gardening teachers work at schools where lessons are mostly given in blocks, and here it is scarcely possible to run the garden with the necessary continuity and involve pupils in the whole range of seasonal activities and cycles. We have to decide how our work with children can 'make sense' in this context. Dissatisfaction quickly spreads amongst them if one group sows and plants in the spring, the next group only weeds and cultivates, and the last can enjoy the harvest. Here again a short-term, project-type approach can be advantageous.

Smaller and larger projects can be especially suitable for work in Class 8 or with upper school pupils, who have usually at least experienced the

A winter project by Class 8 children

primary areas of work in a garden through the year. It is now time for something 'new'. Developmentally it would not make much sense to bore pupils at this age with things they already know well from the past. It is quite common to hear Class 8 youngsters say that gardening is no fun any more, and that they feel they're doing 'forced labour'.

In Class 8 pupils have reached a point where they can work pretty independently and choose a project area themselves, as long as this is properly supervised. There is good reason why a project figures in the curriculum in Class 8. Why not consider, therefore, what areas in the garden might allow for projects where pupils take responsibility? First one needs to clarify what kind of work might be suitable for this, and then let interested pupils choose what they would like to explore. There will usually be a wide range of possible topics: producing creams and ointments, making paper with natural materials, building bird houses and nesting boxes, bottling and preserving garden produce, making a fence, laying down paving on a path, making a garden pond and so on. Naturally one has to see how much time is available and tailor the project accordingly, determine the appropriate size of group on each project, and make sure that the various projects can all be supervised simultaneously.

45

The lovely thing about this kind of learning is that the pupils are almost always very enthusiastic and motivated. They have a sense that their needs are being perceived, that they can use their particular abilities. At the end of the project they proudly present their 'finished product'. To make sure this succeeds it is important to plan and supervise the different stages of the project, discussing every phase of it with pupils. It is also indispensable to have the necessary materials to hand. At this age the youngsters are only just learning to work independently, and one cannot therefore expect them to think through every aspect for themselves yet. If they are left too much to their own devices, they can lose heart because they failed to think things through or something they need is missing, hindering the work and perhaps even preventing it being completed.

In a very small school garden I was working in, project work with Class 8 groups arose quite naturally. In the early years they spruced up old chairs in the gardening room with bright colours, painted the wheelbarrows, built a new garden gate, laid foundations for a small greenhouse, cooked, baked or made ointments. Although such lessons took a lot of extra planning and preparation, it was a great pleasure for me; there were scarcely any discipline issues or problems with concentrating. The pupils are keen to be involved and sometimes you can scarcely keep up with all their ideas, questions and suggestions.

CHAPTER SIX

Lesson Planning and Delivery

No teaching subject is affected by as many external factors as gardening: seasons and weather conditions have a direct impact on the lessons, but the size, location, and arrangement of the garden also have a considerable effect on the form lessons take. Furthermore, there is lots to discover in the garden: tools can quickly become fantastical toys divorced from their actual purpose, while animals such as insects, beetles, worms and birds easily distract pupils from the task at hand. This can mean that distractions and unplanned activities take control, if the lesson is not fully thought through, prepared and well-delivered. It is crucial to think ahead and ask, what could cause a distraction and what should I do about it? Who should be given which task? And finally, the most important question, how do I plan the lesson in a way that engages the children and enthuses them for the tasks?

Equally, hardly any other teaching subject offers such an incredible range of activities. In no other lesson can the themes, as well as the garden and the lesson, be so readily tailored to the individual needs of the children, the school, and personal preferences and capabilities. As a rule, there are far more areas of work in the garden, and theoretical and practical lesson themes, than could ever be covered. There is a danger therefore of taking on too many tasks at once. It is best to have a clearly structured plan, and make specific choices. But it is equally important to allow enough time for the activities you decide on since in this subject it is often hard to calculate precisely what will have to be done when.

6.1 The place of gardening lessons in the school day

Gardening lessons tend to take place towards the end of the school day, at midday or in the afternoon. The pupils will have already done and learnt much by this point and naturally may turn up to the lesson tired, overwrought and lacking focus. There is also a tendency for concentration to flag as the weekend approaches. Teachers should be aware of this and be understanding enough not to set their aims too high at such times.

Try to deliver lessons in a very clear, structured, yet also good-natured way, with humour but without handing over the reins and allowing the lesson to descend into chaos. Key questions for lesson planning include:

❀ What do the children really need in this lesson?
❀ What lessons have they already had that day?
❀ Have they been taught in a more intellectual, theoretical way?
❀ What does their timetable look like overall?

Gardening lessons must be seen in the context of the whole curriculum, with an awareness of the different age-related needs. A long-term, successful teaching plan can be devised on this foundation. Work in the school garden is essentially physical. No project or lesson should be constructed in a purely artificial way. Gardening lessons can offer a wonderful relief for youngsters from the sometimes stressful and often mentally taxing school day.

6.2 A balance between work and reward

Gardening with schoolchildren presents a quite different challenge to the work of the typical gardener. You can't work for two hours at a stretch as a gardener would. While appreciation of nature's imperatives and awareness of the need, in the middle school, to develop perseverance and willpower, are of course key to the gardening lesson, a lesson that is too narrow and monotonous will quickly result in passion for the subject turning to frustration, and an increasing reluctance to participate.

As has already been mentioned, the children will generally already have had several lessons before they come to you, since gardening usually comes late in the day. Tasks in the gardening lesson should therefore be managed in a way that gives the pupils time to relax. There are countless ways to structure lessons in this subject so that work and learning can happen without leading to undue strain and pressure.

It would of course make little sense to lapse into doing things just for the sake of it, just making a lesson 'fun', starting things without ever finishing them or relinquishing tasks as soon as they become too arduous. This would be counterproductive and contradict the pedagogical aims for the middle school as discussed in Chapter 4.

A golden mean is needed, where pupils understand that the necessities of the garden take priority over personal needs, but that work in the garden can also bring its own benefits. The underlying middle school theme of cause and effect is in evidence here: every action has a result. This is not just relevant to work in the garden (good work – good harvest), but can also be applied in the lesson. It is for example sometimes (not always) possible to promise a treat at the end of the lesson, if certain tasks are quickly and satisfactorily completed. Many small things are generally enjoyed by children: tasting freshly harvested carrots, cucumbers or tomatoes together, drinking a homemade syrup, sampling apple purée from their own harvest, or enjoying a small water fight in the garden in summer... If large quantities of any vegetable are harvested, the vegetables can be shared out at the end, or a little guessing game (guess the weight for example) can be played to win them. Nonetheless, we should avoid attaching conditions to everything: the pupils should not take away an entirely reward-dependent attitude to work.

A treat before the summer holidays

If there are time-consuming and arduous garden tasks on the agenda then the children can be split into two teams that switch their areas of work halfway through. This allows the important tasks to be done, but also gives the children variety and will mean they stay focused for longer. It can also be helpful to make the most of situations where there is something interesting to see in the garden by inviting everyone to take a closer look: butterflies sitting on a flower, worms discovered in the ground or compost, wild weeds that return again and again after being weeded, etc.

Pupils will themselves – consciously or otherwise – quite readily find reasons to interrupt the work. There are many things in the garden that can suddenly arouse interest and distract from the task at hand. In such moments it is necessary to sense whether this is timely and helpful or to be discouraged. Situations can arise where children discover or observe something really exciting and are still on topic. These instances should definitely be integrated into the lesson. In other situations pupils develop an intuitive knack for avoiding the task at hand and skilfully inserting breaks into the work. The teacher must of course be on the lookout for this and deal with it in a humorous yet firm manner.

... when the work is done

6.3 Theory and practice

Most teachers of gardening have the justifiable desire to divulge a little 'know-how' in their lessons and sprinkle their teaching with theoretical insights. We should always keep in mind however that learning is most successful in the long term if it is linked to direct experiences and practice. It is not just children who best remember things or situations directly experienced, actually seeing, doing or feeling something. Gardening is in fact a subject where this type of experience is almost automatically available. This wonderful chance should be exploited, rather than attempting to force the experience into a theoretical construct and make a 'classical' lesson of it.

It is of course both possible and to some degree necessary to teach theoretical lessons in gardening as well. These easily arise in connection with practical work and the experiences gained there.

When digging, the teacher can create a moment's quiet to observe the worms that have been turned up and discuss their importance. The growth of plants from week to week can be observed and described while planting seeds, deadheading, and potting. There are innumerable themes that arise out of practical work, for example:

- ❀ Compost and its importance for the garden
- ❀ Care of tools
- ❀ Observing the weather
- ❀ The cycle of the seasons
- ❀ Recognising plants and weeds
- ❀ Soil study
- ❀ Recognising insects and their role in the garden organism

It is generally more fruitful to incorporate themes into the lesson as they arise naturally in practical work, rather than devote an entire lesson to one topic. This is of course different when a 'potato day' or similar is held, when the focus can be on a single theme, both theoretically and practically. In my opinion it is wise to start with doing and experiencing before delving into theory.

Consideration of the theoretical aspects, and writing records in a gardening folder, are particularly suitable for rainy days and lessons in

Leave time for discoveries

winter, when there are few suitable outdoor tasks for a whole group. The question then is how to plan such lessons so that the children can get to grips with them in the absence of the practical aspect (see Recording and bookwork in Section 7.7).

The wonderful thing about working in the school garden is that many things happen by themselves: a bumblebee flies past and settles on a flower, beetles are discovered while weeding, a toad sits amongst the tomatoes in the greenhouse. Or questions are asked when, for example, beautifully flowering weeds have to be pulled, certain materials cannot be put on the compost heap, plant feed is applied or seeds are propagated in seed trays rather than in the garden. It requires a certain openness and spontaneity to recognise and make the most of these moments when pupils' interest is awakened and they are receptive to deeper discussion.

Study of the Steiner curriculum for all the ages through to the upper school shows that many themes surface repeatedly in different contexts. If gardening is considered in this way it can acquire an important support function, awakening an interest in the natural world around us, and its intentional use as crops to sustain human life. The inner stance this cultivates creates a foundation for engaging later with this wide field and its broader implications.

6.4 Making rules

Gardening lessons are a unique part of the typical school day: they do not take place inside a closed space. We are looking at the exceptional situation where the school garden replaces the classroom; it is the largest and most varied classroom imaginable.

On the one hand this offers wonderful opportunities for the form the lesson may take, on the other hand it can make things considerably harder for teachers, unless they are prepared for these realities and have the necessary inner assurance. No other teaching subject offers such a wide, diverse sphere of activity for pupils, both in terms of content and space. The children will frequently be working simultaneously on different tasks in several areas of the garden with different tools.

The teacher faces the challenge of overseeing this situation and attending equally to all the children and their needs. It goes without saying that work in this area can involve certain dangers. If the children ignore the teacher's instructions or use tools incorrectly this can lead – deliberately or accidentally – to damage to the beds and plants, as well as injuries to the children themselves or their classmates. Without getting too anxious, it needs to be clear that garden forks, rakes or spades left lying around in the grass can be nasty trip hazards, while tools carried over the shoulder can hit children behind in the face and cause injury. Stones and clumps of earth thrown through the garden can on occasion hit classmates. It must be made clear from the very beginning that certain behaviour has no place at all in the garden. If children do not follow these rules, a consequence should follow immediately, without hesitation. If the pupils learn that there are no exceptions to these rules, they will quickly adapt their behaviour to them.

These are not the only reasons why it is crucial to introduce clear rules and structures from the very first gardening lesson. Quite apart from the increasing importance and centrality of rules in the middle school, they really make working together in the school garden easier in the long term. It would be impossible to introduce new content and develop further in gardening if every lesson were taken up with recapping rules and methods.

Helping each other as well as safety are important themes in gardening lessons

This basic premise also makes it easier to follow the rules. Rules that are introduced to demonstrate the power of the teacher will quickly be seen for what they are and ignored.

Observation of the social development of children in the middle school quickly demonstrates the significance of rules for this age group: the individual has to discover his or her place in the world, and inevitably boundaries are pushed and re-established. Challenging authority figures (parents or teachers) and constant sceptical querying of things and tasks that were previously accepted without question are simply part and parcel of this developmental stage.

Now and then I hear from colleagues and trainees that they really want to develop and maintain an equal relationship with the pupils, where collaboration is based on understanding and a partnership ensues. This idea contradicts the natural hierarchy of teachers responsible for their pupils' education. Furthermore, this type of 'equality' in a lesson quickly leads to frustration and sometimes even a personal feeling of injury: something is being expected of the children that is not appropriate to their age. This will lead to problems since the pushing of established boundaries is vital for individual development. If clear boundaries are not enforced, pupils themselves will show increasingly inappropriate behaviour that demands boundaries be set.

Parents, carers and other adults are always to be heard complaining about the lack of respect, manners and politeness shown by the young people today. But where and how are they to learn these things when their principal carers avoid setting clear boundaries and dealing with the resulting challenges?

As we have already seen, rules and their consequences should be reasonable to the pupils: it should not be a case of doling out meaningless punishment, but instead of communicating the fact that every type of behaviour has its consequence. It does little good if a pupil is given lines for throwing stones. It makes much more sense for this pupil to clear the lawn in the school garden of stones that might end up in the blades of the lawnmower, doing so at the end of the lesson while his classmates enjoy their harvested produce together.

It can also be productive to warn that the prospect of a treat may vanish if the group completes its tasks too slowly, without concentrating or taking enough care. This instance can be used to illustrate the fact that tending the garden always comes first, before cooking and eating together, for example.

As the pupils get older, in particular from Class 7 onwards, long-practised rules are often readily forgotten: for example, used spades are put away at the end of the lesson but not carefully cleaned first, in the hope that the teacher will not notice and that there may be a chance to get out earlier for break or at the end of the school day. One has to stay alert to such behaviour and not just overlook it. The only thing to do is to send all the pupils back and insist that the lesson will not end until all the spades are clean and hanging in the tool shed. This will generally result in discussions within the group, because some will of course have properly cleaned their spades: this self-regulation is a positive side-effect and often results in such behaviours happening less often in future or even stopping completely.

Once in my lesson, as I later discovered, a pupil inadvertently stabbed the main hosepipe with a garden fork. It was only when I came to water the garden in the afternoon and turned on the tap that I realised what had happened: I was unable to use the water blaster and had to water the garden with a smaller hose. When I asked about it the next morning in main lesson, the culprit came forward straight away. Of course it would not have been right to punish the pupil for his honesty. Yet it would have saved me a lot of effort and time in the afternoon if he had said something earlier. The logical consequence of this was that the pupil had to spend extra time in the garden, where we repaired the water pipe together. This meant on the one hand that he could learn how to carry out such a repair, and on the other hand came to understand the consequences one tiny hole could have. If I had repaired the damage myself without involving the pupil, he (or others from his group) might later have deliberately broken garden rules to see when and how I would react.

6.5 Motivating pupils

Gardening lessons generally begin in Class 5 or at the start of Class 6 and are taught by the same teacher for several years. This makes it all the more important that the introduction to the subject is successful and that the children develop a positive feeling towards the work that will last them beyond the middle-school and teenage years.

At the end of Class 5 and beginning of Class 6 (age 10–12) pupils are full of energy, eager to learn, and willing to persevere. They will gladly get stuck in and enjoy getting things done, happily loading up one wheelbarrow after another or keen to be quicker than their classmates at digging. Now and then pupils of this age will ask whether they can stay behind after class and continue working. Many children have their own plot in their parents' garden at this age.

This age group is ideal for first gardening lessons. The children are physically already able to handle most tools and to work. They also demonstrate an admirable readiness to work, and natural curiosity. If the teacher succeeds in managing these qualities in the right way and awakening interest in the garden and the tasks connected with it, then an important foundation for the coming years has been laid.

It is quite likely that the interest and engagement of adolescents will appear to weaken noticeably during Class 7. This is an entirely natural phenomenon of the first stages of puberty, and the teacher should not take it to heart. It is vital to stress that even if the pupils seem to be increasingly inattentive in lessons and to have lost all the knowledge they once had, constantly chat with their classmates and undertake even the smallest of tasks only with much grumbling and moaning, what they experience in these lessons is nevertheless absorbed, and has a positive impact elsewhere. Parents often mention unsuspectingly that their children – frequently the ones you would not have expected, given their behaviour in the lessons – have spoken enthusiastically about gardening at school, are proud of their harvest, or that they even dig their own plot in the garden at home. It is crucial to keep reminding oneself of this with teenagers and to deliver the lessons with a good deal of humour.

It goes without saying that gardening is a lesson which frequently involves tasks that are arduous, tiring and awkward, and which are increasingly thought of as such in the middle school. Yet this in itself is one of the very reasons why work in the garden should be carried out with this age group (see Chapter 4). It is therefore even more important to structure the lesson in a way that enables pupils to recognise the purpose of their tasks and easily comprehend why they are doing something. There must be no room for any sense they are just being 'occupied'.

Alfred Graf states: 'Adolescents want to experience "realities" in order to connect themselves with the world, the earth and the universe, to become citizens of the earth and feel at home and safe on earth.'[1]

The best remedy for lack of motivation is abundant work. This may sound a little absurd: we are often ready to give in to the children's very convincingly expressed (and often strongly felt) belief that they are hugely overworked. Yet a stringent workload cultivated from the outset turns out to considerably reduce such grumbles and moans. As long as there are tasks to be getting on with, pupils have less time to dwell too deeply on their lack of motivation and succumb to it.

Sharing tasks out (with time indications) at the beginning of the lesson avoids individual children getting out of doing things during the class. As we saw, the mood can often be improved by offering the prospect of a treat at the end of the lesson after completed work, like a homemade syrup or tea together, a small snack of garden produce or a little water fight in hot weather – there is no end of possibilities and it will soon become apparent what each class likes best.

Although the work can be tiring, many pupils in Classes 5 and 6 love sieving compost and moving soil

CHAPTER SEVEN

Planning Lessons for Different Age Groups

Lessons in the school garden can be structured and themed in a huge variety of ways. This in turn makes it especially important to work out which activities are most suitable for each age group. Much care must be taken to decide the way in which specific tasks and long-term lesson topics will be addressed and approached. There are no strict rules or guidelines for this, but if you look into the possibilities for your own school garden and age groups, it quickly becomes clear that certain themes and approaches are more suitable for some age groups than others. Each age group should be presented with new themes and activities so that the subject remains interesting and pupils continue to be inspired and encouraged to develop new skills. Though certain activities in the garden are suitable for all age groups, and others must be repeated every year, a new approach should always be found to maintain children's focus and interest in gardening until the end of middle school.

7.1 Garden plots and beds

Various types of beds are suitable for gardening lessons. Whereas in commercial horticulture the beds are designed to optimise production, gardening lessons require a layout designed for learning. The two most common forms will be discussed here.

Communal beds

The normal practice at many schools is to create communal beds for each class or teaching group, which they cultivate together throughout the season. Each job is carried out by every member of the group together; the group can be divided into smaller units which work on different activities at the same time.

Each group or class is responsible for one part of the school garden. This teaches a communal approach to responsibility for the garden. The children learn that a bountiful communal harvest at the end of the season depends upon everyone making an effort. While they work they continually observe how other group members apply themselves,

A communal bed cultivated by Class 5

and how differently others tackle each task. The best-case scenario is that pupils within the group begin to encourage, correct and help one another.

As schoolchildren enter puberty, they focus less on their surroundings and more on their own feelings and psyche. Working as part of a group or towards common goals can help counter this self-involvement.

Work on communal beds also has downsides. This working model offers pupils many opportunities to avoid getting involved. It is hardly possible for a teacher to engage each child individually in a group of twelve, or remain ever vigilant. The teacher has to rely a little on the children's willingness to work, something which, experience tells us, wanes increasingly with the onset of puberty. Pupils insist on confrontation at this stage and continually test whether teachers are able to meet this.

Work on communal plots must therefore assume more differentiated and individualised forms towards the older end of middle school, to ensure that all pupils share productively in the responsibilities.

I personally believe that work on communal plots is perfectly suited for introducing children to the subject. Children in Classes 5 and 6 can learn basic gardening skills and how to handle common garden tools particularly well on group plots. The advantages of communal work hold true especially for this age group. The teacher will have an easier job imparting new skills to the whole group rather than addressing each pupil individually.

Pupils in Class 5 can begin to grow vegetables together in one part of the school garden in spring: digging over the plots, measuring out beds, marking seed furrows, sowing, planting and tending the plants. In autumn, at the beginning of Class 6, comes the first communal harvest, which can be shared amongst the class and used in preserving and cookery lessons.

Measured out, dug, planted and cultivated communally:
the first fruits of gardening in Class 5

Individual beds

The alternative to communal beds, depending on the size of the school garden, is to give pupils of one or more classes responsibility for their own beds. They can work individually or in groups.

Individual plots reduce the importance of communal activity. In my experience, the two do not have to be mutually exclusive, particularly as I do not recommend individual beds being given out in the first season when the subject is first introduced. Before they work on their own beds, children have to have basic gardening knowledge since the speed and abilities of different children vary considerably and the teacher has to give a lot of supervision.

Children in Classes 5 and 6 are at a stage of development where in general they happily bring strength and stamina to the task at hand, and take pleasure in achieving a tangible outcome. Work on communal beds is perfect for this age group.

From Class 7 onwards it becomes apparent that the pupils find it harder to motivate themselves. By now they are familiar with many gardening jobs which repeat seasonally every year. For gardening lessons to continue successfully these familiar tasks must be viewed and approached in a new and more differentiated way. Individual beds are particularly suited to this purpose. Assigning individual beds allows

Planting onion sets on individual beds in Class 6

pupils to develop a heightened sense of responsibility, and ends all argument about why they are doing certain things.

In February (late winter) you can start by discussing the things to consider when planning a plot: suitable vegetables and flowers, row spacing, the difference between heavy and light feeders, etc. Then the children can plan their plots on paper, before propagation of the first plants in the greenhouse or cold frame, and the preparation of the beds.

This form of bed distribution usually leads to pupils prioritising the work on their own plots each week. But since time may often be left at the end, they can work together communally too, in other areas of the garden. This reinforces the pupils' awareness that their responsibility extends beyond their own plot. They are also taught to help one another when somebody works faster or slower than others or misses a lesson.

The first tasks of spring: everyone helps measure the plots together before they are shared out

An advantage of individual beds is that pupils continually meet the results of their own work. Nobody can hide behind their fellow pupils and claim that others have sown wrongly or pulled weeds badly, worked too slowly or pulled up young plants by mistake.

I have experienced all manner of remarkable things happening on individual plots. Even children previously fairly reluctant to engage in gardening lessons persevere every week with their beds. Often pupils

Class 6 pupils begin to sow using their planting plans

return in their breaks, in free periods, or after school to check their plots and see whether their radishes or lettuces have grown a little, or whether the bed could do with watering.

On one occasion some years ago the gardening lesson was rescheduled for the main lesson period. I waited for the pupils first thing in the morning in the gardening classroom but nobody turned up. I began to get annoyed, as I had never had a group not turn up to a lesson. So off I went to find the children. Unable to locate them, I decided after quarter of an hour to stop being annoyed and spend my time productively in the garden. And there they all were, at work on their beds. They asked in surprise: 'Mrs Kaufmann, where have you been? The tool shed is all locked up.'

7.2 Growing vegetables

The focus of gardening activities in different classes varies very greatly from school to school. This depends very much on the age-groups taught and the school garden itself.

Plan by two pupils from Class 7 for their herb and flower plot,
Two Class 6 pupils tend their beds

In general, cultivating vegetables serves very well as an introduction to gardening. Even if the children have little prior knowledge and have no experience working with tools, quite reasonable harvests will still result. Many vegetables are robust and cope well with 'less than professional' planting and cultivation. Often they can be planted straight into the bed and their relatively large seeds make for easy sowing. Certain other vegetables are also easy to plant once they have been propagated in a greenhouse or cold frame. One approach, which corresponds well with growing seasons, is to begin by planting potatoes and progress to vegetables which require more tender care in sowing and cultivating: for example after planting potatoes, progress through lettuce and kohlrabi, radishes, beetroot, peas and chard, to carrots.

Children also tend to have more of a connection to vegetables than to herbs or flowers. They know at least a few vegetables from shopping for them and eating them, and quickly become curious as to how these grow in a garden. There are still many children from all backgrounds who are woefully unaware of how and where vegetables grow. In the last few years I have encountered many children who were astounded to find that potatoes grow underground and not on a tree or bush. Other children concluded from this that tomatoes must be dug up too. I could list many more such examples.

Since different vegetables can be grown and harvested throughout the season, there is always something new for pupils to discover.

This comparison always surprises pupils

The first vegetables such as radishes can be harvested very early on and immediately sampled. Even children who resolutely refuse to eat vegetables at home will generally relish the opportunity to eat vegetables which they have cultivated and harvested themselves. It is astonishing, actually, how few vegetables some children are familiar with. This is a wonderful opportunity to learn together that nature offers a varied feast: that besides tomatoes, cucumbers, potatoes, kohlrabi, lettuce and carrots there are other vegetables such as parsnips, chard and turnips. Another lesson is the multitude of varieties of each vegetable: butterhead and iceberg lettuce are just two varieties amongst many with varied tastes, shapes, and colours; potatoes can vary hugely in shape, taste and size; and tomatoes are not always red and round.

Vegetables and other cultivated produce make up a large proportion of our daily intake, and it is therefore vital for children to learn where these foods come from and how they are grown. This knowledge will be the basis for them, later, to make their own conscious decisions about what they eat, and understand factors involved in world food production.

The size, location and soil quality of the school garden have a considerable impact on what can be planted. Some schools are fortunate enough to have large plots of land suited to ambitious growing projects. This can raise the issue of what to do with harvested produce over and above immediate requirements. There must of course

Rosmarin

A good exercise for Class 7 or 8 in cold or wet weather: careful study and sketching of plants

be no wasted surplus, as this would contradict the basic principles of the lesson and be ethically irresponsible. There are thankfully many options for making use of extra harvest: weekly produce sales to parents (for example in the afternoon in the school car park); stalls at school fêtes or markets; or a regular supply of produce to the school kitchen. It is a real bonus that many vegetables can easily be conserved or stored for use in the winter months.

7.3 Flowers, herbs, medicinal plants

In some schools flowers are chosen as a crop for gardening lessons in Classes 5 or 6, with the idea that children particularly appreciate the beauty of blossoms. I have already said, however, why I think it is best to introduce gardening by cultivating vegetables.

I myself have found over the last few years that flowers (sunflowers, herbs, certain medicinal plants) are best suited to Class 7. At this age, and with the gardening knowledge already acquired, the children can engage more strongly with specific plants and their uses. To grow flowers, the youngsters should prepare beds individually, in pairs, or in small groups. They can work out in advance, with a little

Planted in spring in Class 5: the first carrot harvest from the communal plot

Flowerbeds are a welcome addition to the garden ...

assistance, how they will make their planting choices: colourful flowers, flowers for bouquets, bee-friendly plants, garden herbs, or plants for tea infusions etc. By Class 7 pupils are able to consider more detailed aspects and factors relevant to their cultivation plans.

Flowers offer many opportunities to supplement practical work with botanical knowledge. It is often assumed that flowers 'are for girls' and that boys will resist this area of gardening. In my experience boys certainly do engage with the practical aspects of flower growing: they enjoy discussing in their groups how much space is needed by each plant and whether all the flowers they want to grow can fit in the bed. There will always be boys who insist that their mother's favourite flower has to be included.

A further advantage of embarking on flower growing in Class 7 is that the children's motor skills will be more developed and they can master the more careful approach required for many summer flowers. It is usually a good idea to propagate most of the annuals in seed trays, to prick out the seedlings and then transfer into pots before planting them in the garden. These are all tasks which differ from that of cultivating vegetables, requiring the youngsters to learn new methods and skills.

... and delight the children more than you might think

7.4 Propagation, direct sowing, transplanting

Some vegetables, as well as all herbs and summer annuals, are best started off in a cold frame or greenhouse rather than being planted directly in the garden. Many species however can also successfully be planted *in situ*.

Several factors affect the decision, a lack of space in cold frames or greenhouses certainly limit the scope of propagation there. Propagation in seed trays, transplanting, and potting requires far longer than direct planting in the ground.

You should also be aware that propagation, with all its necessary stages and processes, is a crucial experience for pupils. The various tasks reveal and highlight each developmental stage from seedling to fully developed plant. The children also learn just how much careful work and attention is required for a blossoming plant or healthy lettuce to adorn the garden.

When certain plants are sown directly in a bed, there is a risk that too much seed will be used and that it will be distributed unevenly. Anyone who has ever sown with schoolchildren will know that even precise instructions cannot prevent mistakes, gaps in the rows, or

seed pile-ups, with much seed wastage. The children also struggle to distinguish between newly sprouting seedlings and weeds. As long as vegetables are sown in rows this can be easily avoided. The problem with flowers and herbs is that they are best planted in groups rather than rows and are more difficult to differentiate from weeds in their early stages. Snails also present a big danger to new seedlings – another reason why propagation in cold frames or greenhouses is preferable.

7.5 Composting

The composting site is one of the most important places in an organic garden. Nothing is as alive as the compost heap. If no cattle or horse dung is available, the compost heap is the most important source of fertiliser and soil enrichment.

The theme of compost is one that surfaces repeatedly in gardening lessons: vegetable peelings might be collected during a group cooking activity and brought to the compost heap, where the teacher can easily clarify what can and cannot be placed on the compost heap. There will be lessons when the compost is turned, mixed, sieved or spread on the bed. The children will see for themselves how collected waste turns into moist, friable and low-odour soil.

Many children have negative associations with all this. They confuse compost with dung, or have encountered bad-smelling, poorly made compost. This makes it all the more important to tackle this theme head-on and convey to children the vital significance of the compost heap.

The compost and its importance for the garden can be discussed at various levels. All classes should engage in practical work with compost: sieving, spreading on beds or collecting plant waste for the compost heap. You must make sure that younger classes are not overtaxed by such activity: filling and moving wheelbarrows loaded with compost can be physically exhausting for the children. The pupils love this kind of work at this age, so it is best to regulate the time spent and the amount carried in each wheelbarrow. In contrast, Class 7 pupils often enjoy this task less, but can now be challenged to handle larger quantities.

Propagation by individual pupils as stock for communal planting of the school garden; many developmental stages can be observed and important processes can be learnt

Sieving compost, digging, using a wheelbarrow: favourite activities for many boys, who like to demonstrate their physical prowess

From the very beginning we should discuss with pupils why there is a compost heap and what happens to the waste there, along with what can and cannot be put on the compost heap, and why. The compost heap provides a lesson in the composting process: what happens at each stage (and at what temperature) and which creatures – worms for example – can be observed in the compost.

The theme can be addressed anew and in more detail from Class 7 onwards (bookwork in winter is a possibility): the idea of the cycle of life – beyond the compost heap as well – some facts and figures of decomposition, the micro-organisms and worms involved in the process. The subject is wide-ranging and diverse, providing much food for thought in lessons.

7.6 Keeping animals

Some schools keep animals: bees, rabbits, chickens and ducks through to sheep, goats and pigs. Sufficient space is the basic prerequisite, but you also need the financial resources, and willing people to care for

Can't do it alone? Work as a team

the animals. Even if animals are kept at only a few schools, they are a wonderful addition to the garden. Animals bring the garden alive and help pupils get on board with the subject because they immediately feel an inner connection with the animals. Most people find it easier to establish a connection with animals than with plants. With children this is particularly noticeable as they approach the animals enthusiastically, watch them, and want to stroke, look after or feed them.

Keeping animals enriches the gardening lesson with animal care activities: children can for example take it in turns to muck out, feed and water the animals. The children often willingly take on responsibilities and make a special effort to do everything well. Pupils who can be difficult to engage in lessons can demonstrate great independence and reliability when carrying out these tasks.

The pupils also directly experience the benefits of animals and their dung in a kitchen garden and learn how a life cycle can and should develop. Rather than creating a 'pet menagerie', careful thought should be given to which animals best suit the particular location and will meaningfully enrich gardening lessons.

There are questions surrounding keeping animals which have far more weight in the school setting than they would on a farm or at home: what should be done with old or ill animals? Will the animals be slaughtered for meat? Will the animals be bred, and what should be done with their young? The emotions connected with these themes and their potential rapid escalation into school-wide hysteria should never be underestimated. Children and their parents need to be consulted to ensure successful handling of these issues.

Death is a difficult subject in our society, and one that is often taboo. In many areas of life (medicine, sport, nutrition) the tendency is to do everything possible to delay natural aging, illnesses and death. Nutritional supplements and a whole range of medicines and operations exist to extend the life-spans of our guinea pigs, rabbits,

A dog can also benefit lessons. This dog has often had a calming influence on children

cats and dogs, without asking whether this is the right thing for the animal.

Keeping animals in the school garden may be the first opportunity for children to encounter questions surrounding death, illness and meat production. These can all provide valuable material for discussion of varying views and lifestyle choices. This discussion must also take place before animals are introduced into the school garden. There are schools where domestic animals (rabbits, goats etc.) are regularly slaughtered and their meat sold to the parents. This can only work if the relevant issues are openly and regularly discussed with the parent community, at parent evenings for example.

A special friendship

Every school manages this discussion differently and decides which activities and decisions require the active involvement and backing of the parent community. Some schools have reported excellent results from keeping animals in the school garden, stating that the children accept all aspects of animal husbandry. Other schools have experienced conflicts whenever an animal is to be put down or slaughtered. Recent epidemics have also been handled very differently. During the bird flu scare, protective parents at various schools wanted to stop their children taking part in gardening lessons because there were chickens and ducks in the garden.

Keeping animals at a school requires careful prior planning and consideration: the gardening teacher is taking on another huge responsibility. The animals must be looked after at the weekends and on school holidays too. It might not be too much of a disaster if plants are not watered once or twice, but animals can't be treated like that.

Sometimes children and their families offer to adopt the animals and look after them during the holidays. This is not entirely reliable as the adoptive family could pull out at any time and scupper the teachers' holiday plans or force them to spend large amounts of time organising alternative care. The amount of time required will depend of course on the type and number of animals. We must also ensure that animals passing from the care of one person to another continue to be fed correctly. Animals can quickly become ill if they are fed the wrong thing or the wrong amount of food.

The reverse is another possibility: the gardening teacher can 'adopt' animals, offering space for them and looking after them during school time. Once there was a caretaker at our school who could no longer look after his rabbit. The rabbit was given a hutch and run in the school garden and was cared for in lessons. The caretaker would then look after the rabbit at weekends and in the holidays. There was also a pupil who lived close to the school and would spend a lot of time looking after the rabbit at weekends. At another school an old man living nearby was given land for his animals. In return he looked after the school's animals at weekends and in the holidays for many years.

At our school someone always set up a beehive in the garden so that we could have bees without myt having to look after them. Sadly, the tending of the bees was often rather unreliable, meaning the joy of seeing the busy creatures at work was short-lived. It is necessary to consider how long-term and reliable care for bees can be guaranteed. If you ask around in your own local area, you may well find a beekeeper who is only too happy to house his bees in your garden, as there are often few locations available for beekeeping.

Making apple rings together

Reliable care is one aspect of keeping animals, another is the weighty matter of financing this. Besides necessary start-up costs, barn and fencing etc., there are running costs. The animal feed must be partly or entirely bought in (grain, hay, straw). Alongside regular treatment (immunisations, worming etc.) unplanned veterinary bills may arise. Insurance may be a good option, but the school should agree to meet the running costs, to avoid living in uncertainty as to what next year may bring.

Only actual experience will show whether keeping and looking after animals is a sustainable activity at your school. All the issues should be carefully thought through in advance to prevent possible failure. It is not pleasant, or a good learning experience for the pupils when animals become ill or have to be sent away because they are not being looked after properly.

7.7 Autumn and winter activities

Winter is a time of withdrawal – not just for vegetation but also for us. Just as farming work used largely to be done in the warmer months, while the cold, dark winter was used for inside jobs and craftwork, and to rest and prepare for the coming season, so this time also plays a special role in gardening lessons. When activities in the garden come to an end in autumn, there is suddenly time available for other things.

There is no end to possible lesson activities in the winter months. It is up to each teacher to pursue his or her own skills and preferences in shaping this period in an interesting and creative way, while still as far as possible relating it to the whole cycle of the gardening year. The activities presented below are therefore just some examples to kindle your own ideas.

Candle dipping

This is a much-loved activity in many schools. It relates to gardening in so far as bees are vital to the garden, and these industrious creatures

Dipping candles as winter activity in Class 6

may actually be kept in some schools. Even where this is not the case, candle dipping is often a firm tradition. This is partly due to its almost therapeutic quality: it exerts a magical attraction for children. The quiet atmosphere, and wax fragrance in a comfortable, warm room (because of the heat from the candle-melting equipment) enhances their perseverance. They can continue the activity over several weeks without ever tiring of it. This is an excellent thing to do during Advent, in harmony both with the reflective mood of this time of the year and with candlelight's special significance in the dark winter months.

If you teach regularly in Classes 7 and 8 (age 12–14), you quickly find that qualities such as perseverance, care, patience, composure and concentration are not the prime attributes of this age group! And yet it is precisely these qualities that the curriculum seeks to nurture now. Candle dipping is therefore an excellent activity at this age, offering opportunities to practise these, and even to enjoy doing so. Whereas a teacher's exhortations to work carefully and with concentration will often otherwise lead to expressions of exasperation from pupils, candle dipping itself teaches them the need for this. If they rush, if their hands are not steady or if they lose concentration, this will become immediately apparent in the candle itself. Most pupils quickly realise this, and adapt their behaviour accordingly.

Pupils usually get very involved in this work

The result of industrious work over many hours

A distinctive aspect of candle making is that it always leads to success, irrespective of any previous craft skills the children have (or have not) developed. Even if the finished candles vary in shape and size, and are not always perfectly straight or smooth, they can all be used and will all burn equally well. This is beneficial for children with poor motor skills who have difficulties in other handwork or craft subjects, and gives them a very valuable experience of success.

But this success has to be well prepared by a careful introduction first. The teacher must convey that candle making is a special and valuable thing, and that there are high costs involved both in the equipment and in the beeswax itself. In the current situation where so many bees are dying, the raw material of beeswax is a very precious commodity.

It is good therefore to set certain 'professional standards' when dipping candles. This can be done by getting the children not only to produce candles for themselves but to make them for sale. This means not only that their candles must be of good quality, and that they must make an effort to ensure this, but that the candle sale can also cover most of the costs of the activity. An incentive to ensuring the children engage fully with this project is to insist that they first make beautiful candles for sale before they can make their own. Candles produced by pupils can be sold at winter bazaars at relatively high prices.

Given the high costs of this activity, especially if all children make several candles for themselves, you might consider asking the pupils to pay a small amount towards it, such as the purchase price of the wax they have used (calculated by weighing the finished candles). This has further benefits too: they can practise weighing, and calculating prices, and work out the change due to them. This will also help them to be careful about the quantities and sizes of candles they need or wish to give as presents, and can enhance the care they put into the work.

Naturally this activity could also first be done on a 'small scale', using simple wax-melting pans and improvised equipment. The important thing is to ensure that children have enough space to work and do not have to wait around too long between each dipping. If pupils are standing there holding their candles they can get restless, and this will easily detract both from the mood and the quality of the candles, especially if they start getting up to mischief with the wax. We should always try to remember the pedagogical point of an activity. In many places candle dipping is offered as a fun activity in kindergarten or at school markets. If it takes place in lessons, though, it should cultivate a different quality of attention.

Candle making has technical aspects that cannot be further elaborated on here but that you need to be aware of. Do seek advice from experienced colleagues.

Cooking and preserving

The produce from your school garden may include all kinds of vegetables as well as fruit, herbs or medicinal plants. You may sometimes have large quantities of produce, more than can be consumed in lessons when you cook and eat together with pupils. When designing and planning the garden, make sure there is sufficient diversity of produce to include vegetables for storage, some of which you can process and preserve in the autumn and winter to ensure tasty supplies are available through the cold months.

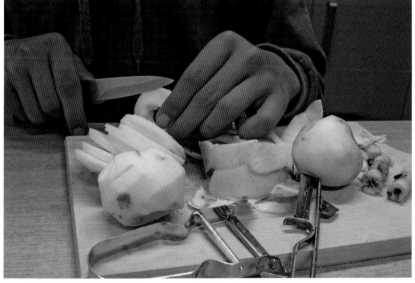

Processing your own produce is work the children love and gets through large quantities

There are endless possibilities here, for instance:
❀ Juices from apples or quince
❀ Quince bread
❀ Apple sauce or dried apple rings
❀ Jams and jellies
❀ Pressed oils
❀ Mustard
❀ Preserved cucumber, beetroot or squashes, etc.

If you have, say, a store of potatoes, carrots, pumpkins, onions, beetroot or cabbage, you can conjure a tasty feast at the end of a lesson. Look in recipe books or ask your colleagues for ideas.

Pupils of all ages, both boys and girls, love this kind of activity: slicing fruit and vegetables, stirring the pot and seeing how, in next to no time, tasty things are created from produce they have spent so much time and effort cultivating in the garden. Processing harvested produce and eating together are, if you like, the reward for all the work they've done, and mark a meaningful conclusion to it.

Alongside this, they learn basic cooking skills. Often nowadays children no longer witness daily cooking at home, nor does everyone sit down to share a meal. Even in the upper middle school some children may not know how to use a knife properly, peel an apple or dice an onion. Many pupils only meet certain types of vegetable or ways of preparing them in school lessons. It can be eye-opening for them to realise that produce they cook or preserve themselves tastes better than ready meals or fast food.

Cooking and preserving can be done at all ages, though the stages of a process need to be adapted to the different ages and skills of pupils. For instance, a Class 6 doing these activities for the first time can easily peel apples in a large group and slice them to make apple rings, or slice and pound cabbage to make sauerkraut, or cut vegetables for preserving or for making a large pot of soup. In the process they learn simple and easily understood skills which they can draw on later for more complex processes and recipes.

In Class 7 and 8 the tasks can become more differentiated – for instance in individual work following a recipe, or making jams or jellies in twos, or cooking in a small team while the others are working outside, making a meal for all to eat at the end of the lesson.

In Class 8 likewise, one can place an emphasis on cooking and preserving, as a logical conclusion to the preceding cultivation work and harvesting. Thus they learn what all their work has led to: a wealth of products created from their own garden.

At the school where I work, we made a virtue of necessity here: cooking became a fixed part of the gardening curriculum since the school garden is simply too small to accommodate all the classes. There were not sufficient age-appropriate tasks for Class 8 to further develop

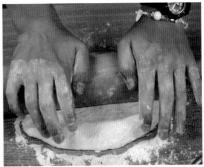

Top: *Pupils in Class 8 cook in teams with various recipes*
Bottom: *Every pupil 'creates' their own preferred pizza*

the skills and experience they had had so far. Initial attempts at cookery in lessons – with very spartan equipment – immediately triggered a rush of enthusiasm. Both girls and boys were equally keen, and there were no discipline problems whatsoever, or adolescent moans. We now have a well-equipped kitchen and cookery takes place in two six-week blocks in alternation with handwork and craft. Cookery lessons are carefully structured to increase in complexity, starting with smell and taste tests, followed by lessons on herb salts and spices, through making herb butter, steaming vegetables, cooking simple soups or baking bread together, to working individually according to chosen recipes.

If one runs ongoing cookery lessons in a class, it will be necessary to ask some questions of principle about the ingredients used: should we only use produce from the school garden or is it alright to buy in ingredients too? If so, do we only buy organic products or can we also use conventional ones from the supermarket? While we should of course try to make conscious choices in this respect, and highlight these choices in our lessons too, the pedagogical aim of the cookery lessons is the main thing to consider. What produce is available in our school garden and are there sufficient quantities to do a broad enough range of cooking? How much money is available to buy in other items? Large amounts of food are needed for one double lesson if all pupils are going to get involved. This costs something. Even if parents can make a small contribution to costs, this alone will not cover the outlay, and we will have to consider whether local and organically grown produce is affordable. In my view the most important thing today is that children get *any* opportunity to learn cookery and to sample food they themselves have cooked. It would seem wrong for costs to be so prohibitive that this opportunity is denied them.

If cookery and food preserving is to be included in the curriculum or given a more emphatic place there, you will need some basic equipment of course. But it is astonishing how little you need to make a start: a two-ring stove, some crockery and cutlery, a few cooking pots – and you're off! It is worth appealing to parents, who will very likely find all kinds of useful things they don't need, perhaps even preserving jars. After a one-off appeal that I launched ten years ago, families still regularly leave me clean, empty bottles and jars with twist-tops at the door of the gardening room.

Making herb salt

This activity is worth mentioning specifically since it introduces some valuable qualities and is almost always a firm part of the gardening curriculum. It is quick, easy and cheap. The school garden will have a range of herbs, and coarse sea salt can be purchased. All you need apart from this are enough pestles and mortars for all participants.

The nice thing about this activity is that you can vary the composition of herb salt depending on the herbs available, and it will always produce a tasty result. You can experiment at will with lovage, parsley, celery leaf, thyme, rosemary, summer savory, sage, basil, chives.

Certain wild herbs or flowers can be used too. In the process the children will become familiar with the various herbs and their smells and tastes, and see that even if their taste or smell is too intense on their own, they become tasty when processed like this with other herbs. All children like herb salt.

In a relatively short time (one double lesson) you can produce a fair amount that can be used throughout the year in lessons. And there will still be enough left over for every child to take home a little bag of their own salt.

The technique is simple and can also easily be done in lower classes – a spontaneous activity for a rainy or winter day perhaps. The amount of herbs and salt used can be tailored to individual children, the slower ones being given less and the quicker ones more, so that all finish more or less together. The activity is perfect for middle school age since it requires some exertion, perseverance and care. The children discover how hard it is to grind and sieve the materials to produce a relatively small quantity of herb salt. Some teachers use electric grinders or coffee mills to hasten the process (for instance if larger quantities are needed for sale). But in general it seems preferable to do the job the 'hard' way so that all pupils are involved at once, and can fully connect with the work.

Children are usually very keen to participate, and enjoy the smells of chopped, crushed herbs. They compare the contents of their own mortar with those of their neighbour to see whose salt is finer and who is making fastest progress. At the end of the lesson it is very enjoyable to have a festive cracker each with butter or slices of tomato or cucumber so that they can try out the herb salt they have made. If they are allowed to take some of the salt home, this will usually only be small quantities which children often guard like a treasure. Parents repeatedly tell me that the children only allow the herb salt they made in the lesson to be used on special occasions.

Making Advent wreaths

At this time of year the garden is largely dormant and has been tidied up for winter, leaving time for making Advent wreaths in lessons. A direct relationship to outdoor work can be established by, say, using self-cut willow rods or other branches to make the inner roundel.

Making Advent wreaths with children from Class 5 to 12

You may have enough fir branches on the school grounds, or you can go foraging for it in the woods; or otherwise ask your local forestry office whether they can let you have some cheaply. Sometimes parents or teachers may have some pine or fir tree branches from their garden.

The 'classic' wreath can be made with pupils in a great variety of sizes and for a range of purposes – for use at home, in the classrooms or for sale. It is of course rather special if the wreaths used at school or at home were made by the children themselves.

But it requires good planning. There is only a short period when wreaths are made, and the work cannot be done too early as otherwise the wreaths will have lost all their needles halfway through Advent. Since gardening lessons usually only happen once a week, the wreaths should be of a size that can be completed in one double lesson. For larger wreaths it is better to have two children working together (with one holding the branches while another winds the wire around them). This can also be a good idea for younger pupils who do not yet have the strength or big enough hands to hold the branches and wind wire at the same time.

Naturally you will need large quantities of fir branches cut to the right size, something that there will not be enough time to manage in the lesson itself unless several children take turns to work on one wreath. If they are making wreaths to take home, the teacher will need to cut the branches before the lesson. Or perhaps you can 'borrow' pupils to do this as a special project. Making the frame or roundel also takes time and must likewise be done in advance.

But Advent wreaths do not have to be made only in gardening lesson time. One year, for instance, I invited almost every class to send me two pupils during main lesson to make a wreath for their classroom. This created a wonderful working atmosphere in which the older ones gave warm encouragement to the younger children.

Since making Advent wreaths coincides with the time when candles are also being made at many schools, some teachers make special time available for it during an afternoon or even on a Saturday so that all those interested (children, parents and teachers) can participate. At other schools this activity is offered during the Christmas market.

Recording and bookwork

As described in detail in Section 6.3, we can ask how often and in what form children should receive more theoretical instruction as part of gardening lessons. Some topics and situations offer themselves very naturally to written recording.

In gardening lessons the prime focus is not on bookwork. And it is therefore a good idea for every child to have a folder or looseleaf binder to which new pages can be added as and when. This folder can accompany gardening throughout the year so that you are not left at the end with half-filled workbooks. This also makes it easier to get pupils to redo work if they did not take enough care the first time. In addition, photocopied sheets can be added to the folder (for instance seed charts etc.).

It is best to keep these folders in the garden teaching room, organised according to group. Since gardening lessons usually only

happen once a week it may often happen otherwise that children leave their folder in the classroom or at home, especially as they are not used in every lesson. This makes it difficult to get written tasks done retrospectively and to keep an eye on which child has failed to do this.

Bookwork is suitable for recording topics that the pupils have engaged with practically the previous season. As mentioned elsewhere, children should initially connect with experiences and inner pictures rather than more abstract themes – which, on this foundation, come later in science lessons in the upper school.

It is useful to write about ordinary gardening tools at a relatively early stage, examining their function in detail: comparing forks, shovels and spades, different lengths of handle and ways of handling, and, say, why a pitchfork cannot be used for the same jobs. Likewise one can compare secateurs and grass shears or different kinds of hoe and rake. The nice thing about this is that one can see from the very shape of a tool what purpose it is designed for. Children can explain and describe their observations and ideas verbally before one gets them to carefully draw and caption these tools. Depending on their age, they might add a short, self-formulated text to the illustrations.

Composting has of course a very important place in the school garden. Here too we can explore the topic in more detail and record this in writing, describing everything that can be included in a compost heap, the processes involved there, the creatures that aid the process of decomposition, and the special role of worms etc.

Other, more general themes can be studied, such as:
- ❀ The seasons (temperature, position of the sun, plant growth, bird migration etc.)
- ❀ Weather observations (temperature, precipitation, wind)
- ❀ Herb lore (related to smell and taste tests)
- ❀ Plant observations with drawings

The title page of a gardening book, designed by a Class 6 pupil

Children can also write down recipes for products they have made in lessons:

- ❀ ointments and creams
- ❀ herb salt
- ❀ syrup
- ❀ jams and jellies
- ❀ apple puree

These are only a few ideas, of course. It all depends on what you have done in the lessons, your own interests and expertise, as well as the range of produce in the school garden and the work you do there. When choosing a topic for bookwork it is worth considering how it relates to the practical work that children have been doing.

Care of tools

Good garden tools are fundamental for successful gardening. The school garden therefore needs sturdy shovels, spades, forks, etc. in sufficient quantities, even if purchasing them is expensive. Cheaper

Writing about tools: work done in the winter in Class 6. Left: The pitchfork. The long handle and thin tines makes it easy to pick up straw, twigs, hay, etc. It is not suitable for digging and turning sods. Right: The shovel. Like the pitchfork a shovel is used for picking up earth, sand, gravel, etc. Its broad blade is suitable for this work. Its long handle avoids having to bend too much

Heading towards the 'tool-cleaning' site

An enjoyable activity: pupils first estimate then weigh the harvested produce

plastic-and-metal alternatives will not long survive frequent handling by pupils.

Expensive tools ought to last, but even when urged to clean and put away tools carefully after lessons, pupils will rarely do this to a professional standard. It is therefore important to keep reminding them that the 'throw-away' mentality so common today has consequences and increases costs. This can be highlighted, for example, in an annual tool-care project.

Winter lessons can be used to check all the tools in the shed, to scrub the blades of spades and shovels and if needed de-rust them with emery paper, to oil tools and if necessary repair or replace handles. Garden shears can be overhauled, tool hooks cleaned, and everything properly re-arranged and organised.

All pupils can be occupied together in these tasks and even if one or other of them starts complaining, they may also realise that a little more care with tools during the growing season would have helped avoid some of this work. This form of communal tool-care develops the children's awareness that they are responsible for the tools they use in the garden, and they will use them again next year.

Other winter activities

I have not listed all the possible autumn and winter activities. These will depend on your own skills, the nature of your school garden, the size of the teaching room and its equipment and how much funding you have.

You will certainly have more ideas than can be realised in the available timetable! Conversations with gardening teachers in other schools will also expand the range of possible projects, and suggest ways of putting them into practice. At many schools the following are undertaken:

- ❀ Pressing walnut oil
- ❀ Making mustard
- ❀ Building nesting boxes
- ❀ Making bird-feeders
- ❀ Sorting self-harvested seeds and filling seed packets
- ❀ Making and sticking on seed labels
- ❀ Making tea mixtures
- ❀ Processing herbs, roots and blossoms to make tinctures, creams or ointments

Another creative activity – though it requires sufficient room and the right equipment – is to make paper with natural materials. These can include stinging nettles, straw, blossoms, hay, grass, leaves, chives. You can make very beautiful works of art in this way.

CHAPTER EIGHT

Gardening Lessons in Different Schools

No other subject is so dependent on external conditions as gardening. The position and size of every school garden will vary enormously, as will equipment, facilities, premises and finances. The region and location will also play a role. Planning will be affected by climate and varying school holidays.

We can be sure that there is no danger of 'uniformity' in provision. Naturally this is harder for gardening teachers new to the field. They cannot simply adopt approaches their experienced colleagues have introduced elsewhere, but must find their own way in each situation, discovering what is desirable and possible at their particular school. On the other hand, this means there are countless possibilities for working individually and creatively. Actually, from a Waldorf point of view it is very beneficial for teachers to form a strong personal connection with the specific situation in which they work and with things they wish to impart to children.

It is not easy to take on the teaching of gardening at a school, especially since in most cases one is working more or less alone and there is no one with whom to discuss things or share experiences and tasks. A certain inner strength is needed. But if things work out, gardening lessons and the school garden can enormously enrich a school and the school community, becoming a kind of advertisement for it. Especially today, with such lively debate on environmental and ecological issues, nature conservation, and consumer attitudes, and with long waiting lists for urban allotments, gardening as a school subject ought to be taken up consciously again and integrated more fully into the curriculum. Work with pupils in the school garden offers a wonderful opportunity to give the next generation positive experiences and knowledge of nature. Few any longer can acquire this as a matter of course, though it is very important for our well-being and for nurturing the earth in future.

8.1 The size and design of the garden

In most cases we are unlikely to have an 'optimum' size of garden at our disposal. Schools can count themselves fortunate if there is a suitable plot on their site or nearby. If it is possible to select a suitable site and design it as you wish, it is important to have enough space and areas of activity for all the pupil groups, but to make sure, also, that staffing is adequate to supervise them.

It best of course if a school garden offers scope not just for a 'classical' vegetable plot but has a diversity that allows pupils to engage with many different aspects of gardening, including corners for nature observation and reflection, as well as plenty of space to move.

No school garden is the same as any other: they range from tiny plots squeezed in between blocks of flats to large acreages with animals and orchards. In some cases there are bees, chickens, ducks or rabbits, sometimes even goats, sheep, pigs or other domestic animals. Some have garden ponds, greenhouses, herb spirals, insect hotels, cottage gardens, fire sites, dry-stone walls, nesting boxes, etc.

Really there are no limits; but we should be clear what we are trying to achieve with our garden design. We have to consider pupil ages and numbers, and what their real needs are – in other words what are the activities and tasks best suited to the ages for which the garden is intended? Properly run gardening lessons are ultimately not simply a matter of 'nature exploration' or just a time to stroke pets.

In general, a school garden can be a place where older pupils, teachers and parents can also meet and talk and which, above and beyond lessons, can act as a uniting element for the school community as a whole. This aspect should not be underestimated. The more a garden is integrated into the school as a whole, the more it will awaken awareness and interest in all those involved in the school. Over time this reciprocal action can strengthen and enrich all of school life, besides creating real support for the gardening lessons.

Above all a school garden should be planned and realised in a way that caters for work with children, in a sense adopting the function of a classroom. The groups working there need to be able to move around it freely and easily. For instance it is a good idea to make sure paths are wide enough for pupils to pass each other with tools and wheelbarrows, without getting in each other's way or encroaching on beds. The tool shed should be accessible, well laid out and clearly organised since so many people will be involved in using it and keeping it tidy.

As mentioned earlier, it is very important to have a wide enough range of possible activities in the garden to fulfil various pedagogical aims. But at the same time the garden should be clearly organised and structured, with its primary areas easily apparent. It will then be easier for pupils to see and accept where they can move around freely or where they need to take more care – and what kind of behaviour is permissible in which part of it. In a clearly ordered garden the teacher can more easily keep an eye on all groups or individuals at once, even if pupils are working in many different places. It is good to remember all the creative ploys pupils are capable of if they think they are unobserved and can withdraw into little corners and hideaways.

Whatever your site allows, and whatever ideas and wishes you try to realise in designing the garden, you must be sure it can be cared for and cultivated continuously. The main growing period is in the summer holidays, so work in the garden at this busy time must be done without pupils. This must not lead to a wilderness springing up and the spoilage of crops the children have sown and cultivated. There is nothing more frustrating for them than to come back from the summer holidays and find that the work they did last year has been more or less all in vain.

It takes time to establish a new garden. If, in addition, you are starting as a new teacher at a school and face new tasks in many areas, try not to take on too much at once. A garden has to grow and develop. And only gradually as you work with the children will it become apparent what is useful and necessary where, which beds are best suited for growing particular crops or which areas of the garden acquire primary importance for cultivation and should be given special attention.

The title page of a gardening book

8.2 Organic gardening and use of biodynamic preparations

Nowadays it should be self-evident that a school garden is run organically. Besides the fact that themes such as sustainability and ecology are global issues, it would be pedagogically counter-productive to try on the one hand to enhance pupils' awareness of the living earth and all it provides us with, and at the same time to intervene in natural life cycles with pesticides and artificial fertilisers.

Coming generations will be confronted increasingly by grave environmental problems and man-made natural catastrophes. A primary task of gardening lessons therefore is to encourage pupils to look for

103

ways through such problems, seeing how they can be surmounted through sustainable lifestyles and working in harmony with nature.

The biodynamic approach, an early and still very innovative form of organic agriculture, was introduced by Steiner at the beginning of the last century. As long ago as that, farmers were already noticing a worrying trend: soil and crops were declining in quality. In his Agriculture Course Steiner also noted that food produced by orthodox means would soon no longer contain enough of the nutrients human beings needed.

The course of eight lectures he gave in Koberwitz (now in Poland) in 1924 to a small group of anthroposophical farmers who had approached him with their questions, created the foundations of biodynamic agriculture with its associated preparations.

Unlike other organic methods, biodynamic agriculture goes beyond orthodox scientific explanations to include cosmic forces as an indispensable aspect of all life and growth. It seeks to integrate them in agricultural processes to nurture the health and life forces of the soil and the plants growing in it.

There is no scope here to detail the principles of biodynamic agriculture or to describe the various preparations. These matters require careful study of the Agriculture Course and regular dialogue with experienced gardeners or farmers. And yet a gardening teacher at a Waldorf School ought certainly to be familiar with this theme since it forms the basis of an approach which gives full, devoted attention to the earth and its needs, in the same way that the Waldorf curriculum attends to the needs of child development. It is also true to say that the life forces of plants are weakening noticeably and that we should do all we can to strengthen them wherever possible.

There are no general rules about the extent to which making and applying the preparations in the school garden should involve pupils, and whether or in what way this should be discussed in lessons. There are many different views on this subject, resulting in different practices. There are schools where certain aspects of biodynamics are taught in lessons, and also realised in practice, whereas other schools prefer gardening teachers to undertake such activities alone.

Certainly careful thought should be given to the age at which one might introduce this to children, and in what form it would be appropriate. This is a sensitive area that could easily be misunderstood, especially near the end of middle school, and made to seem ridiculous. The principles of biodynamic agriculture are complex, and difficult to penetrate even for many adults. They cannot be understood without much study, and a willingness to accept underlying spiritual realities. We should therefore formulate any explanations in an age-appropriate and limited way. Often simple answers will be enough to satisfy initial interest. Rather than offering abstract, intellectual ideas we need, as in all subjects, to connect with the children and their feelings.

Some children will be familiar with homeopathic remedies in the form of small white globules, and may have been given them for particular ailments. I drew on this once as a comparison, when a Class 6 child asked how the preparations work, saying that they give the soil and plants the strength needed to stay healthy, like homeopathic granules. This was a perfectly acceptable explanation for these pupils.

Even in Class 9 it is too early to go deeper into these matters. During their work experience the youngsters may well witness the production and application of biodynamic preparations, and will record this in their work experience diaries. It becomes clear however that as yet they are not ready to understand the principles underlying these procedures.

Besides use of preparations, the influx of changing 'qualities' from the cosmos also plays an important role in biodynamic gardening. This depends on the changing positions of moon, sun and planets, with influences affecting the development of leaves, blossoms, root or fruit. For instance, the day on which, say, a root plant or a leaf vegetable are sown, cultivated or harvested, affects the growth and quality of the crop. Researchers such as Maria Thun have spent decades investigating and recording these influences. The Thun family publishes a calendar each year with guidelines for the best days for sowing, cultivation and harvest of different crops.

However it is more or less impossible to coordinate gardening lessons in the school day with the constellations and their rhythms. If a particular day is perfect for sowing carrots but it rains heavily during the lesson, this activity would be problematic. Yet the same group will not come back for another week, and there may not be another suitable 'root day' that coincides with their lesson. Class trips, holidays, weekends and excursions make planning still more complicated. In the end we have to give priority to the educational aims of the gardening lessons and the activities associated with them. Sometimes there will be a chance to work in harmony with these qualities of the cosmos but this principle should not be so strictly adhered to that classes fail to experience and learn all the necessary seasonal tasks, leaving the teacher to do much of the work alone.

8.3 The teaching room

Again, available premises will vary enormously from school to school, depending also on whether the garden is on the school grounds or located somewhere else. Anything from a normal classroom through converted stables or heated greenhouses to romantic garden sheds with a wood stove can serve as a teaching space. Necessity is the mother of invention, and this sometimes gives rise to very cosy and useful spaces which pupils particularly appreciate.

The room needs to serve a variety of purposes, and have enough tables and chairs for all so that activities can continue in winter or in bad weather. The room should not just be for theoretical lessons but must be flexible and large enough for practical work to be done there too, such as making bird feeders or Advent wreaths, or for communal cooking and eating together, or candle dipping. Washing facilities will be needed too. It is very helpful if the room has a cooking stove and even a small range of other kitchen equipment.

As time continues, tools and teaching materials are likely to 'collect', so if possible you need enough storage and shelves. The more space available, the wider the range of equipment, and the more flexible, creative and interesting lessons can be. This also makes it easier to adapt them to the needs of different age groups.

8.4 Tools and materials

The equipment and materials needed for gardening lessons make it one of the most expensive items on the curriculum. And yet if a school is committed to including it, you can start off by improvising a lot of what you need, and gradually increase resources over time. However, schools should realise that this situation cannot continue indefinitely, and that a good range of appropriate tools will be necessary.

Costs will naturally vary depending on the emphasis of gardening lessons. It is important for there to be enough tools so that all the children in a group can work at the same time. You will have to have plenty of the most important tools (hoes, forks, spades, rakes, etc.) and enough wheelbarrows will be needed too. All tools necessary for running a vegetable garden professionally ought to be available in some form or other.

It is helpful if there are always plenty of work gloves, in a range of sizes. We can't always ask the children to work without them, even though it is often good for them to experience the soil and plants directly. Many jobs are easier, and are done better, without gloves. If pupils are asked to bring their own work gloves, there will be complications when they 'forget' them at home. The same is true of wellington or rain boots. Here, though, there is not much point in procuring 'community boots'. It is easier to ask the parents or children to leave boots at school, so that they all have a pair and do not fuss about wearing 'disgusting' ones that others have worn before them.

Der Spaten

Genau wie die Grabegabel hat der Spaten einen kurzen Stiel mit Griff, so dass man sehr gut beim Stechen in die Erde kraft ausüben kann. Der Spaten hat ein schmales, scharfkantiges Eisenblatt, mit dem besonders gut gerade Kanten abgestochen werden können. Außerdem bietet sich der spaten gut

The Spade

Like the garden fork, the spade has a shaft and a handle so that you can get a good grip on it when digging. The spade has a narrow, sharp-edged iron plate at the end, with which you can dig very straight edges. The spade is also good for turning over the soil

107

There is no end to the tools and materials needed for gardening, though this will also depend on the size and position of the school garden, the number of lessons, and the teacher's energy and creativity. Materials will be needed too for lessons during the winter months, especially if these include practical activities of various kinds.

In most cases, though, equipment is added as the lessons themselves develop. It is hardly possible to realise every potential idea and project in the first few years. As time goes by it will become clearer what emphases are appropriate for the teacher, the structure of the lessons and the school itself.

If equipment is lacking to begin with you can try asking around in the school. It is astonishing what 'treasures' a parent may sometimes find lurking at home and gladly donate: crockery, electric kettles and cooking pots for communal cooking; preserving jars, bottles, drying equipment and slow cookers for conserving fruit and vegetables; flower pots for thinning and transplanting, etc. With any luck you may find parents willing to help fund a refrigerator or stove, garden tools or kitchen cupboards.

An annual budget has to be made available for the subject, since, each year, you are likely to have to buy in seed, seed potatoes, replacement equipment, young plants, potting soil and certain fertilisers.

8.5 Teaching rhythm and lesson frequency

Again, it is difficult to make general rules. As we saw in Chapter 4, the focus of this subject is on middle school although this may vary along with the number of classes taught. If possible the subject needs to continue over several years to bear the best educational fruits and cover the full scope of activities. In practice gardening is undertaken at least in Classes 6 to 8.

Sometimes however gardening lessons are taught in limited blocks rather than throughout the year. This cannot do full justice to the aims of gardening lessons, despite offering interesting content and an intensive period of learning. Project-oriented work can be undertaken in this way, but it fails to address the primary concern of gardening lessons in the middle school, which is ultimately to offer a counterbalance to the turbulence and volatility of incipient puberty at this time. This happens through an experience of the regularly recurring seasons and the continuity of gardening work over many months. No other subject requires such persistence and rigorous attention to conditions that are simply objectively 'given' (weather, climate, growth of the garden).

If gardening is taught in lesson blocks, it loses its intrinsic purpose for the pupils. They may ask why they should prepare the soil in spring and sow seeds if they can't experience the growth and harvesting of crops. Likewise it is much harder to kindle their interest in weeding and other cultivation work if they themselves will not be reaping the harvest of this work in the late summer and autumn. They can easily feel they are being exploited. Yet it is precisely in the middle school that youngsters form an (often unconscious) desire to do meaningful work and be involved in purposeful activity. Often they will ask at this age, '*Why* are we doing this?'

For these reasons it is definitely a good idea for them to engage in gardening in a weekly rhythm throughout the year. The weekly lessons should last at least for a double period (or longer). Single lessons are too short to allow a meaningful structure of activities. An initial explanation of what you will be doing that day, then finding work clothes and tools, the work itself and then tidying up at the end, cannot all be fitted into a single lesson. Nor will this allow for reflective moments, of great pedagogical importance, to observe and experience phenomena in the garden. In single lessons too there is not enough scope to develop the perseverance that is so important a part of these lessons.

8.6 Group sizes

Teachers of every subject like to teach groups that are as small as possible, to be able to address pupils' individual needs. Anyone who teaches a practical subject knows the importance of this. Only when a teacher has enough one-to-one time to show children how to take each step at their own pace, can this kind of lesson run smoothly and satisfactorily.

The size of a group is especially important in gardening since children may be spread out and engaged in many different activities. Groups vary in numbers from school to school, depending of course on staffing, organisational and financial factors, as well as on the class size. Groups vary in size from 10 to 20 pupils. While one group does gardening, the others are involved in subjects such as handwork and craft.

Gardening teachers find that they cannot really take account of individual needs in groups of more than about 12. Since the work in this subject is primarily practical, and the children will often be working at different places in the garden, it is extremely important to keep all areas in view. If a teacher loses sight of individuals or if the size of the group means they always have to all do the same work together, some children will start to feel frustrated. Situations can quickly develop where they lose interest, get distracted or begin to be disruptive. Especially in the school garden – the biggest and most diverse classroom that there is – there are countless opportunities for pupils to 'disappear' and withdraw from what is going on.

It is important also that there are enough tools for everyone in the group. If this is not the case, it is well-nigh impossible to ensure that all are engaged in meaningful activity, which in turn gives rise to boredom and complaint, and sometimes to them finding other activities not connected with the lesson at all.

The size of the garden will also determine the maximum group size. Even if there are enough tools for all the pupils, many activities can only be done with a certain number of children. It is inconceivable to have 20 children 'wielding' a spade at the same time, or to get them all weeding at once, let alone have them all trundling wheelbarrows around.

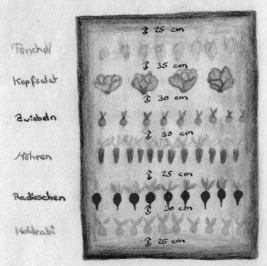

Beetplanung 2011

Fenchel

Kopfsalat

Zwiebeln

Möhren

Radieschen

Kohlrabi

↕ 25 cm

↕ 35 cm

↕ 30 cm

↕ 30 cm

↕ 25 cm

↕ 30 cm

↕ 25 cm

*Class 6 child's
vegetable bed
planner*

CHAPTER NINE

The Skills of the Gardening Teacher

> It is clearly necessary for particular people to begin to
> shape a specific piece of land in their own individual
> way. Only then does a garden organism develop, so
> that pupils can engage their will with its needs and
> requirements. This organism has to become a real
> individuality, something tangibly experienced rather than
> just a cleverly devised plan.[1]

This chapter may strike many readers as too critical, but my comments
here are based on some schools' problematic involvement in this
curriculum subject. Repeatedly I have encountered an assumption that
gardening lessons could somehow be catered for as a sideline. To put
it more cynically, there will be people at the school who have 'some
kind of gardening experience' and *simply need* a couple of hours extra
teaching time.

And yet every subject is offered to pupils with particular pedagogical
aims in mind. If a school is convinced of the importance of a subject, it

has to ensure that it is taught properly by qualified teachers. If this is not the case, we have to ask why this subject is being offered in the first place.

Nor should a school make value distinctions between different subjects – for instance because some are more exam-relevant than others – and therefore fund and staff these areas better than art or craft subjects. A careful and fair analysis will show that these latter disciplines help pupils to develop many vital skills and abilities which, when they reach upper school, enable them to engage with more motivation and focus in intellectual or theoretical issues.

Gardening is a subject that requires a wide range of teaching skills. As stated, the school garden is the largest and most diverse classroom any school has. A gardening teacher not only has to be fully conversant with all the jobs and tasks required in a garden but also keep an eye on all the pupils in a group who may be spread out across a wide area and involved in many different jobs at once. They all need appropriate tasks with corresponding guidance and instruction.

To fulfil these requirements, it is very important that a teacher has a proper training in both horticulture and education. It is not by chance that the majority of gardening teachers have first trained as gardeners, farmers, agriculturalists, landscape gardeners or similar, and that this is also a requirement for the profession (see the survey in the Appendix). In a faculty meeting with teachers of the Stuttgart Waldorf School in 1920, Rudolf Steiner remarked on suitable teachers for gardening: 'it is a different situation with the gardening class. That needs someone who really understands the subject.'[2]

Often there are teachers interested in gardening who assume that they have learned enough about this in their spare time to take it on as a subject. Of course this may be enough to run successful, small-scale garden projects, but to structure the whole gardening curriculum through several school years you will probably need proper training.

In the first Waldorf School in Stuttgart, Steiner noted critically of the gardening teacher at the time:

> What I have seen indicated that he does not have
> sufficient practical talent so that the children could not
> do their work well because he himself does not have an

eye for what the craft demanded ... The worst thing was
that he simply had no heart for his work.[3]

While gardening lessons in middle school do not aim to make
children into 'little professionals' or fill them up with theoretical
knowledge, pupils very quickly sense whether a teacher has mastered
the subject and can engage authentically with the tasks involved. This
does not mean that the gardening teacher must always be able to answer
every question – for after all, as Steiner stated, a 'good teacher' is always
learning. Yet it is essential for a teacher to have a real connection with
the subject: a degree of assurance and basic knowledge, and to be at
home in the garden's huge and continually changing 'classroom'.

Imagine what effect it has on pupils when the gardening teacher is
there with them in the garden but is not really sure what needs to be
done first in spring – what plants should be sown and at what intervals,
or which tool is best to use. It is even worse if the teacher cannot
distinguish young vegetable seedlings from weeds so that a potential
crop is eliminated during hoeing. It is very disappointing indeed for
pupils if lack of such knowledge means that the work of many months
is all for nothing.

If the teacher has inadequate knowledge and skill, thus leading to a
great many errors, the whole pedagogical aim of gardening lessons can
soon become questionable.

But please do not misunderstand me. No one can know everything
from the outset. Gardening especially is a field where one's knowledge
continually develops with the work of each new season. A great deal
of the success or failure of gardening will depend on the location
of the garden, climatic conditions and soil quality. The teacher will
need to gain intimate knowledge of the garden and its distinctive
characteristics. There is hardly any other field of work where so many
variable factors depend on the site and local conditions.

The profession of gardening teacher offers a very diverse and
exciting range of tasks – great scope for creativity and development.
At the same time this involves certain requirements: the teacher
needs to feel an inner relationship with nature and its manifold
interconnections, and should always be willing to encounter new
situations or learn something new. Much patience and persistence

is needed, and without these qualities it is will be very hard to run a school garden successfully.

Every potential gardening teacher should realise that they are likely to be the only one at the school, and therefore bear great responsibility. It will be their task to represent their subject both to the faculty of teachers and to parents. Only rarely will they have a colleague with whom to discuss and share their work.

They also need to know that gardening lessons cannot always follow a prescribed plan, but are affected by a variety of circumstances. What jobs are done and when, depends on the weather and the state of growth of plants and crops. It may well be that you have to go and water the garden at the weekend, or find time to cut grass, weed or thin certain plants because this cannot be delayed until another lesson comes round. And of course the garden cannot remain untended for too long during holidays in spring and summer (see section 10.6). The role of the gardening teacher involves tiring physical work and requires fitness, perseverance and energy. By no means can all the work be done in lesson time, and therefore the teacher needs to be fully committed to the garden.

CHAPTER TEN

Gardening Lessons in
the Whole School Context

Few school subjects offer so many opportunities as gardening for activities over and above lessons, or for integrating into other aspects of school life. But this unique quality in turn requires active efforts to establish gardening as a serious part of schooling. It can easily happen that the gardening teacher has so much to do in daily lessons and garden work that he or she loses regular contact with the other teachers and with parents. This can lead to lack of insight on the part of many on the faculty, or parents, as to the value and diverse nature of this subject. I have often been astonished to find colleagues or parents suddenly standing there in the garden in summer and gazing at the colourful blossoms and vegetable beds with admiration, seemingly unaware before that such a thing had long existed at their school.

The work needed to run a school garden means boredom is most unlikely! Besides the gardening and teaching work itself, there are all the general tasks of paperwork, meetings and so on. But alongside this, in the same way that a class-teacher has to organise class festivals, class trips, parents' evenings or plays, the gardening teacher must get involved in other activities if this subject is to become firmly established.

Because of the financial outlay needed for gardening, some schools look a little askance at it and – if it does not seem to be making a full and attractive contribution to school life – may add it to the list of possible cutbacks. Yet the school garden offers so many opportunities for enriching the community as a living sphere where people can connect with each other. In the sections below we will look at some of the ways to integrate gardening into the whole school community, and see that this can at the same time improve our work and make it easier.

Building a greenhouse in the school garden with the help of parents on a Saturday workday

10.1 Garden workdays with parents

A school garden will always involve jobs that are difficult to complete in lessons alone – whether building a fence, cutting down a tree, doing repairs or undertaking larger building projects. Either there will be too little space in the timetable for such activities, or the children will not be strong enough or have the necessary skills. Some projects simply cannot be undertaken with larger groups since individual pupils would not receive enough guidance or instruction from the teacher.

Since it is usually too expensive to employ people to do this work, it is a good idea to hold garden workdays with parents several times a year. The parent body may often include people who have the necessary skills, and are glad to offer their know-how and tools.

Community workdays can have positive social outcomes and help get parents fully behind the gardening lessons. The teacher, who often works alone, will find it very valuable to gain parents' appreciation and understanding. Besides ensuring bigger jobs get tackled that might otherwise remain undone, workdays establish good relationships with parents. Specialist teachers, unlike class-teachers, rarely have much direct contact with parents, except perhaps when misbehaviour makes a phone call necessary. It is very beneficial therefore if they can meet up and work together voluntarily now and then, without focusing on any specific need connected with the children.

To mobilise enough parents, it is important to publicise workdays well in advance at parents' evenings, in school newsletters or on posters. If the workday can become well established it will engender good will and much interest. Many parents may keep returning faithfully, supporting the work over many years.

Each workday has to be well planned and prepared. The skills of participating parents are likely to vary greatly, along with their speed of work, which makes it hard to predict how things will go. But there must be enough tools and materials ready, rather than wasting time and energy by having people go to look for these. There must also be someone who knows what needs to be done, who is able to instruct and direct others. If the gardening teacher does not oversee this, someone who can do it must be found ahead of time. Otherwise chaos will reign and people will feel frustrated. It is good to put a realistic limit on the work so that those involved feel a sense of achievement at the end of the day. This will encourage them to participate again in future. It may also happen that, as the day passes, some of your helpers have to leave, and that there are only a few left by the end to finish the job.

The workday should be enjoyable, relaxed and nurture a sense of community, rather than being too pressured. A convivial break with refreshments is part of this: drinks, fruit, cakes, sandwiches or, in cold weather, a pot of hot soup. Your helpers will welcome this and it will also be a small expression of thanks to them for their efforts.

Much can be achieved on a workday. Over the years we have pulled down and repaired fences, re-roofed the garden shed, laid drains, built a greenhouse, etc. New paths can be paved, water pipes laid, insect hotels or herb spirals constructed, or ponds can be dug. There's almost nothing that a group of parents can't do. Someone amongst them is likely to have the skills you're looking for, and be willing to offer them.

10.2 Fundraising

Gardening is well suited to fundraising at Christmas, Easter or autumn markets, or at a summer plant sale. Summer flowers and vegetable plants as well as crafted or cooked produce such as beeswax candles, herb teas, herb salts, jam, apple juice, bird feeders, nesting boxes, pickles and preserves, are all suitable. Production of saleable items belongs intrinsically to gardening and can enhance pupils' own respect for and appreciation of the subject. They see people willing to spend money on 'their' produce, and this fills them with pride. They also discover how such sales support further gardening work, through purchases of items necessary for activities.

Above and beyond this there are other reasons for holding markets several times each year: to awaken the school community's awareness of the subject and to interest other classes, teaching colleagues and parents. At a market they can suddenly realise the work that is going into the garden; a glimpse of what happens in gardening lessons which otherwise often remain more or less invisible to many.

Gardening lessons often seem to be at one remove from the rest of schoolwork and we have to make efforts to integrate it and include it in people's minds. Fundraising at regular markets through the year can change people's perceptions, suddenly giving rise to discussions with colleagues or parents who have not previously given much attention to the school garden.

These regular sales also broaden the range of possible gardening activities. Depending on the size of the garden, and the number of available lessons, it can be useful and necessary to make products for sale.

It is important for pupils to see that they are not just working 'for themselves' within small and limited confines, but that their work is

Two fathers getting involved in a garden workday

Class 6 boy at the annual autumn bazaar selling candles

useful and that larger quantities are really needed. This also gives them a first taste of the amount of work needed (say in market gardens or farms) to produce enough to earn a living.

It is quite a different matter if, rather than just preparing a few trays of seedlings for one's own bed, this is done in large quantities for a plant sale. Here too the pupils see the need for care and precision, since otherwise the end product will find no purchaser and their work will have been in vain. As puberty begins, pupils find it increasingly difficult to make an effort, and so this is precisely when it makes sense to get them to take care with what they do, not just for their own sake but for others.

Sale of summer flowers and vegetable seedlings

If lesson time allows it, and enough equipment and seeds/materials are available, it is an excellent idea to grow more flowers and vegetable seedlings than are needed for the school garden. Pupils have to work hard, and feel themselves involved in bigger production sequences than if they are growing plants only for themselves or for the garden. Many parents are very pleased to come and buy vegetable seedlings –

Young plants raised and potted for sale

lettuce, cucumber, tomatoes, kohlrabi, courgettes or peppers – along with all kinds of summer flowers, especially since they know their children have been involved in growing them. Prices are also cheaper than in the local garden centre. Again this highlights the work going on in the school garden.

The garden at the school where I work is of moderate size and therefore cultivation is likewise on a smallish scale. But we can never exactly calculate the quantities needed since germination rates can vary greatly. We have to plan in an extra allowance for this and sow larger quantities than will eventually be used. If this means we have more seedlings than we need, we can sell them to parents and staff.

Plant sales in recent years have become a regular feature of our work, so that parents now ask when they can purchase seedlings, and this in turn leads to a warm relationship: throughout the growing season parents report back to us on how big these plants have grown, how well they are doing and when the first flowers appear.

Pupils therefore see that their work has real value, and that people come to the school especially to purchase the plants they have raised and potted. They discover that their work is important beyond the context of lessons, and the pride they feel in consequence motivates them to work with special care. It is easy to explain to children that only strong, healthy plants can be sold. They are also motivated by seeing that the money earned from these sales benefits the garden and therefore ultimately them as well. In a sense this brings us full circle to show that seeds, pots, soil and tools have to be paid for, and therefore all harvested produce from which the children directly benefit involves high costs. Naturally these sales cannot cover the whole cost of gardening work, but they offer pupils an insight into why they should handle seeds, plants and tools with care.

Pupils themselves can take on the sale of plants and produce during certain lessons, two of them being assigned this job at a time. This is a lovely opportunity for them to work in a familiar environment yet in 'real' conditions, serving customers and calculating prices and the change required, without worrying too much that this has to be done 'perfectly' straight away. Parents will usually have enough patience and understanding to cope with children's mistakes and help put them right.

10.3 Parents' evenings

As mentioned frequently, gardening is a subject where we should intentionally cultivate a relationship with the wider school community since it can otherwise remain more or less invisible in the school. Gardening does not lead to performances or presentations at monthly gatherings, so it is important for parents to get some insight into it by other means. Parents' evenings are particularly important here, offering a chance for the gardening teacher to talk about this work and its importance for child development, as well as the ways in which it has value for the learning of other skills and abilities. At the same time one can of course describe what the children will be doing in the garden throughout the year, and what they will learn. Little anecdotes and examples of the work you have been doing can make this all more vivid. And your presentation might include a little introductory tour of the school garden too.

The most important parents' evening will be the first in the year when the class is going to begin gardening, before they embark on this lesson. The teacher can acquaint parents with the range and diversity of the subject and kindle their enthusiasm for it, ensuring their positive and committed support and good collaboration over several years.

Of course the teacher should prepare the presentation well and make a confident impression, offering clear insights into how gardening responds to the children's developmental needs. New teachers may often not be sure how to introduce themselves and their subject at a parents' evening, not yet having experience of how class teachers run their parents' evenings or how other teachers present their subjects. It is important therefore to be clear yourself about what you regard as important aspects of the work. It is helpful to write down what you see as your educational aims, how this will inform the way you run the lessons, and how you want to present all this. Then it is a good idea to clarify with the class teacher how long you can have in the meeting. If you are still unsure about your presentation, you could discuss this with more experienced colleagues or with a mentor.

Like children themselves in lessons, parents should feel enthusiastic and gain a full and vivid picture of what their children can expect in the coming years. If you can awaken their understanding, curiosity and enthusiasm for gardening, this will stand you in good stead in the future since, even if indirectly, they will communicate this attitude to their children at home.

The better the first impressions parents take away about this subject the easier it will be in future to get their active support and involvement in workdays, or in helping out with watering or weeding in the holidays. Transparency and regular contact with parents will prevent any misunderstandings or wrong ideas circulating. And if you do ever have problems with certain pupils that can only be sorted out by involving parents, it is good if they already have a clear idea about the subject and the personality of the teacher.

10.4 Website

Most schools have a good website where they present their approach to education along with highlights from various subjects, as well as announcing diary dates and events. It is an excellent idea to include

123

a section on gardening, with helpful text and photos. It is a good opportunity to support your work and cultivate more understanding for it both amongst prospective and current parents.

In the busy working week it is easy to forget to update the site with dates for plant sales and workdays etc., as well as featuring past projects with text and photos. All this gives a vivid and tangible sense of school gardening activities.

10.5 Working with colleagues

How often do colleagues come along to see what is going on in the school garden or ask about your work? It happens, but it will require work if you are going to awaken their interest. Often, too, the garden is not on the school grounds but some distance away, and so it takes more time to get there. Most of your colleagues will be so busy with their own work that they don't have much time or interest for other areas of the school. As for every subject, it is important to nurture awareness amongst the faculty of the school garden and the work done there. If other teachers have an awareness and regard for the subject they will be more likely to support investment in it, or take an interest in major changes and decisions affecting it.

So why not occasionally invite your colleagues to visit the garden? A faculty meeting could begin with a tour of the garden. Many teachers will even enjoy getting involved for short periods: sowing seeds in trays, thinning young seedlings or candle dipping in winter, and this will give them insight into what you are doing.

Whether in a tour of the garden or in communal activities of this kind, you can tell your colleagues what each age group is doing, though it is also nice if they find out by asking you why you do particular jobs with different classes.

Some while back I got my colleagues to sow seeds in trays and small pots at the beginning of a pedagogical meeting. It was interesting to see how much they enjoyed this and how it kindled lively discussion between them. Some found it painstaking and difficult, and one almost lost patience, saying he would not take part in such a thing again! Others persevered with patient stoicism, placing each seed separately in a single pot. A few weeks later I took the trays and pots with me to the teachers' meeting and showed my colleagues the results of their work. It was astonishing to see how differently the seedlings were growing, although all the teachers had been engaged in the same task.

Quite often your fellow teachers will behave in ways rather reminiscent of your pupils, with a similar kind of group dynamic! They too will have their own individual difficulties with different tasks, and can therefore gain more understanding of what it is like to be a pupil in that situation, as well as recognising the educational benefits of engaging with it.

You can also display or offer produce from the school garden at the weekly faculty meetings: candles during Advent, jams or jellies, bird feeders, the biggest marrow in the garden, a big bunch of summer flowers, seedlings for sale or for a donation towards gardening expenses.

The school year often seems to fly by, with no end of pressures and things to be done; and yet it is still worth reminding your colleagues about the school garden, and keeping it in their awareness, nurturing increasing interest in the subject.

Despite doing this, some colleagues only appear in the garden after years have passed. Some time ago, on a beautiful, fine day, we decided to hold our middle-school faculty meeting in the school garden. On arriving there a French teacher called out in astonishment – 'Ah, here is the school garden. That's what it looks like. May I look around?' I asked with some perplexity if he had never visited it before. After all, his department has windows that look directly out over the garden. His answer was, 'But you never invited me!' This showed me, once again, how much effort is needed to awaken colleagues' interest, and that you cannot rely on this happening by itself.

10.6 Care of the garden in the holidays

This can be problematic since school holidays happen at very unfavourable times in the cycle of the gardening year. In the Easter

Garden workday in the summer holidays

holidays there will usually be seedlings in the greenhouse that need tending, but the summer holidays are the biggest obstacle. These weeks come right in the middle of the fastest growth period for most crops in a school garden.

Gardening teachers cannot do without a vacation. At the end of a year it is important for them, like everyone else, to recoup their strength and energy for the next school year. But nor can the garden, into which so much effort has gone, be left to go wild, with crops spoiling or drying out. When the pupils return they will rightly want to reap the rewards of harvest, and the whole gardening curriculum involves 'purposeful' activity. If the garden is neglected in the school holidays, pupils will wonder, again rightly, why they worked so hard there in the first place.

But there are creative ways to deal with this apparent dilemma. At parents' evenings, or in a circular, we can ask if there are any parents who live nearby who would be willing to water the garden. In the past, several families together have drawn up a 'watering plan' with each family taking on a limited part of the task.

In the middle of the holiday period one can hold two to three 'workdays' with parents and children. One can also encourage all pupils with their own individual beds to come along on one of these days, if they are not away at the time. I have found that this works well, and that parents do not object but in fact accompany their offspring and get involved as well. However, it involves a fair amount of preparation since it is a good idea to get parents to confirm their children's attendance in writing.

These garden workdays allow the gardening teacher to work with children and parents in a much more relaxed atmosphere than is usually possible on an ordinary school day. A little midday snack and drinks can help make the occasion very enjoyable.

There are some schools where garden care is taken over by someone in return for payment so that the teacher concerned is then free of all responsibility. At other schools the gardening teacher cares for the garden throughout the holidays, and has a longer Christmas holiday instead.

If lessons and the garden design allow this, it is also possible to plan crop planting to allow for holiday periods. This means that the main harvest period comes before the summer holidays, and that afterwards you only plant crops that need scarcely any tending during the holiday. But unexpected weather conditions may interfere with these plans, and then you would have to alter your sowing and harvesting times.

10.7 Funding gardening lessons

Gardening involves a good deal of expense as we have seen, especially when introducing this subject into a school for the first time. A plot has to be acquired and developed, and a large number of tools will be needed, as well as a multifunctional teaching room with sufficient space.

As indicated already in previous chapters, costs can be saved by getting the school community involved in setting up and equipping the garden. It is actually beneficial if the garden develops slowly and with the help of many people. This will usually make everyone value it more.

When a garden is being newly established, pupils of older classes especially can get involved in the work, gaining useful experiences in laying paths, building fences and so on.

It will be necessary to undertake careful costing and budget planning. It would be unwise to think that you can do all the work yourself from school resources, and it is very unlikely that all you need will be donated.

You might consider approaching relevant foundations for specific building or other set-up projects, though this will require some research.

Apart from initial investment, there will be ongoing running costs. Besides the salary for the gardening teacher, there will be the regular cost of materials for seed, building projects, purchase and repair of tools, and materials for winter lessons. Some expense is certainly needed to ensure lessons are engaging and diverse.

As we have seen, you can cover some costs by selling produce grown in gardening lessons or other items – seedlings in spring, and harvested produce in the autumn. Sale items can include school-made jams, honey, ointments, juice or candles.

CHAPTER ELEVEN

Working with Other Schools and Further Training

As already stated, gardening work will take a different form in every school. Since the outer circumstances will vary so greatly in every instance, gardening teachers need to make decisions tailored to their own situation.

A few large Waldorf Schools may have more than one gardening teacher – a 'department' if you like, where projects and developments can be discussed. As a lone teacher you may feel uncertain to begin with about the best way to proceed, or where to find the necessary information, whether in relation to representing your subject to the faculty and making the case for more or better equipment, or as regards purchasing tools and seed at economical rates. There will often be no simple answer to many questions, and you will have to find the solution that best fits your circumstances.

New gardening teachers would be well advised to contact teachers of their subject at other schools in the area and maintain this contact on a regular basis. You can help each other and suggest ways to tackle problems, as well giving and receiving very practical support: exchanging plants and sharing useful contacts.

Gardening teachers at Waldorf Schools in Germany hold an annual, one-week gardening teachers conference in January, planned, organised and taking place in different regions every year. These conferences are an important hub and professional development resource for gardening teachers, where you can build up contacts and attend a wide range of lectures, seminars and practical courses.

Gardening teachers without a 'classical' Waldorf teacher training may need to consider how they can best acquaint themselves with Waldorf principles and practical approaches to the subject. This basic knowledge is very useful in developing the work in a consistent and successful way through many years. If possible it is worth attending general Waldorf seminars or subject-specific courses alongside your teaching work. Your school will have information on what is available in your area.

Appendix

Gardening lessons in Waldorf Schools: an overview

Gardening lessons at Waldorf Schools are founded on Waldorf pedagogy and are an integral part of the curriculum.

This work therefore focuses on pupils' developmental stages and needs, and on the whole context of the natural world.

Pupils should discover and experience the beauty and diversity of nature, and learn to perceive its many interconnections.

Through developing insight and creative, nurturing work in the garden, pupils develop a capacity for judgment and a sense of responsibility.

The school garden is created as an environment that offers experiences of diversity, beauty, purpose and meaning.

This gives rise to a sense of reverence and gratitude towards Creation.

Attentiveness and awareness are awoken for the earth and the fact that it needs the respect and care of humankind.

This leads to new and necessary cultural impulses for nurturing and preserving our existential foundations.

(Formulated during a gardening teachers' conference)

Survey of gardening in Waldorf Schools in Germany

In the autumn of 2008, Gerhardt Stocker, tutor in gardening at the Institute for Waldorf Pedagogy in Witten/Annen, Germany, sent a questionnaire about gardening lessons to all German Waldorf

Schools.* The 71 replies were evaluated and the findings were presented at the gardening teachers conference in 2009.

While the survey gives only a general idea of the situation, it does reveal clear tendencies, fairly accurately reflecting the picture apparent at the annual conferences and regional gatherings.

Since it would exceed the scope of this book to present the findings in detail, the most important points have been summarised below to help new members of the profession and those making decisions related to gardening in schools.

Age in which gardening lessons are largely held

- ❁ The survey showed a strong emphasis on Classes 6–8 (age 11–14).
- ❁ At 97.3% of schools surveyed, the lessons are given in Classes 6 and 7.
- ❁ 91.8% continue these lessons in Class 8.
- ❁ 42.5% continue the subject to Class 9 and 27.4% to Class 10.
- ❁ Gardening lessons were given in the lower school (Classes 1–5) in only one school, and in Classes 11 and 12 in 4 and 3 schools respectively.

Group sizes

Of 63 replies to this question, only 1.6% (2 schools) undertake gardening lessons with the whole class, although this does not clarify the number of pupils. In 25.4% of schools, the subject is taught in half classes. The great majority of schools (71.4%) teach gardening in class groups split into 3. (Note: German Class sizes can be over 30 pupils.)

Lessons given throughout the year or in blocks

In middle school (Classes 6–8) there is a marked emphasis on lessons throughout the year. In Class 6, 55 schools offer weekly lessons,

* Despite the survey only covering Germany, we include this summary in the English translation of this book, as it shows some interesting facets.

whereas lesson blocks are given in 10 schools. In Class 7 there is a similar picture: 49 schools offer lessons throughout the year while 8 give it in shorter blocks.

Lessons throughout the year also predominate in Class 8 (39 schools). However, the ratio shifts increasingly. In Class 8, only 20 schools offer gardening blocks. In Classes 9 and 10 the majority give the subject in blocks. It is unclear whether replies relate to farming work experience (Class 9) and the grafting block (Class 10) or whether they refer to gardening lessons separate from this.

The school garden

Of 70 replies to this question, 47 schools have gardens on their own grounds, while 23 have plots at distances of up to 5 km (3 miles) from the school.

Of 58 school gardens, 31 (53.4%) have areas between 0.1 and 0.5 ha (0.25–1.25 acres), while 11 are between 0.5 and 1 ha (1.25–2.5 acres), and 9 gardens are over 1 ha (2.5 acre) in size.

Of 67 schools, 46.3% keep animals in their garden. In 9 schools, three or more species of animal are kept.

The teaching room

Except in one instance (from 67 replies to this question) all schools make dedicated teaching space available for gardening. Over half (57.4%) have their own premises within the school garden. In 72.7% (from 66 replies) gardening teachers have their own cooking facilities in the teaching room.

Farming work experience

This happens at 69 out of 71 schools, and in 82.6% of the latter in Class 9.

In 52.2% of cases (from 67 replies) the work experience lasts three weeks. In 25.4% it takes two weeks, and in 11.9% four weeks.

In 25 schools (36.2% of 69 replies), the work experience is undertaken in small groups; and in 23 (33.3%) pupils are sent to farms on their own or in pairs. 18 schools (26%) undertake the work experience with a whole class.

The grafting block

The grafting lesson block is not, or is no longer given at two-thirds of schools (67.6% from 71 replies). Where it does still happen, it is taught mainly in Class 10 in small groups, for one week on average.

Employment of gardening teachers

Two thirds (67.6%) of gardening teachers (from 68 replies) teach a full workload, while 16.2% (11 teachers) work part-time or more. Just under half (46.4%) of teachers teach gardening exclusively (from 69 replies).

Over half of gardening teachers (57.2%) who teach other subjects too, teach gardening in 75% to 98% of their timetable (35 replies).

In 18.8% of cases (88 replies) teachers said they had trained in a farming and/or gardening profession, and 75% stated they also had training in Waldorf pedagogy.

Notes

1 A History of School Gardens

1. For the historical background in Germany, see Winkel, *Das Schulgarten-Handbuch,* pp. 4, 9, 17f, 22, and Gebauer, Michael, 'Der Schulgarten als Ausdruck des Verhältnisses von Mensch, Natur und Kultur' in Pütz & Wittkowske, *Schulgarten,* pp. 76, 78-80.
2. Mackensen, M. von, 'Zum Gartenbau' in Lange, *Pädagogischer Gartenbau,* vol. 1, p. 9.
3. Steiner, *Faculty Meetings,* meeting of July 30, 1920, pp. 152, 149.
4. Notebook of Frl Michel, quoted in Lange, *Pädagogischer Gartenbau,* vol. 1.
5. Krause, *Gardening Classes at the Waldorf Schools,* and Richter, *Pädagogischer Auftrag und Unterrichtsziele,* pp. 339f.

2 The Experience of the Natural World

1. Pütz & Wittkowske, *Schulgarten,* p. 50.

3 Why Teach Gardening in Schools?

1. Pütz & Wittkowske, *Schulgarten,* p. 44.
2. Birkenbeil, in the Foreword to Kaiser, *Vom Schatz im Acker,* p. 2.
3. Ibid.
4. Giest, Hartmut, 'Kategoriale Bildung im Schulgarten,' in Pütz & Wittkowske, *Schulgarten,* p. 21.
5. Steiner, *Practical Advice to Teachers,* lecture 11 of Sep 2, 1919, pp. 149f.

4 Gardening and Adolescent Development

1. Richter, *Pädagogischer Auftrag und Unterrichtsziele,* p. 339.
2. Ibid.
3. Kaiser, *Vom Schatz im Acker,* p. 3.
4. Steiner, *The Child's Changing Consciousness,* lecture 5 of April 19, 1923, pp. 109f.

6 Various Teaching Methods

1. Graf, Alfred, 'Der Gartenbauunterricht als Symbiose von Gartenbau und Unterricht,' in Lange, *Pädagogischer Gartenbau,* vol. 1, p. 17.

9 The Skills of the Gardening Teacher

1. Mackensen, M. von, 'Zum Gartenbau,' in Lange, *Pädagogischer Gartenbau,* vol. 1, p. 9.
2. Steiner, *Faculty Meetings,* meeting of July 30, 1920, p. 152.
3. Ibid, p. 149.

Bibliography

Kaiser, Christoph (ed.), *Vom Schatz im Acker: Schulgarten, Landwirtschaft, Ökologie. Naturerziehung an den Waldorfschulen Tübingen und Heidelberg,* Tübingen 2003.

Krause, Rudolf *Gardening Classes at the Waldorf Schools,* Biodynamic Farming and Gardening Association, USA 1992.

Lange, Peter (ed.), *Pädagogischer Gartenbau: Gartenbauunterricht an Rudolf-Steiner-Schulen,* Auslikon 1993.

Pütz, Norbert & Steffen, Wittkowske (eds.), *Schulgarten- und Freilandarbeit: Lernen, studieren und forschen,* Bad Heilbrunn 2012.

Richter, Tobias (ed.), *Pädagogischer Auftrag und Unterrichtsziele einer Freien Waldorfschule,* Stuttgart 1995.

Steiner, Rudolf, *Agriculture* (CW 327), Biodynamic Farming & Gardening Ass., USA 1993 (also published as *Agriculture Course,* Rudolf Steiner Press, UK 2004).

—, *The Child's Changing Consciousness* (CW 306), Anthroposophic Press, USA 1996.

—, *Faculty Meetings with Rudolf Steiner* (CW 300), Anthroposophic Press, USA 1998.

—, *Practical Advice to Teachers* (CW 294), Anthroposophic Press, USA 2000.

Thun, *The Maria Thun Biodynamic Calendar,* (times in GMT) Floris Books, UK annual.

—, *The North American Maria Thun Biodynamic Calendar,* (times in EST/EDT), Floris Books, UK annual.

Winkel, Gerhard (ed.), *Das Schulgarten-Handbuch,* Seelze 1997.

Index

More books for Steiner-Waldorf Teachers...

The Tasks and Content of the Steiner-Waldorf Curriculum

Edited by Kevin Avison and Martyn Rawson

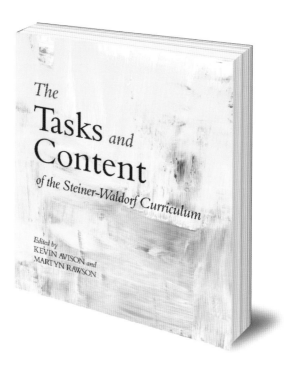

This handbook is indispensable for all Steiner-Waldorf schools and teachers.

As well as describing the content and methods of the Waldorf curriculum, this book provides a clear overview of the ideas behind the approach. It includes: a summary of the ideas underpinning this unique form of education, a survey of child development in relation to the curriculum, a description of key elements in the Waldorf approach, sections on evaluation and assessment, self-management, Early Years education, a horizontal curriculum for Classes 1 to 12, a vertical curriculum for each subject.

florisbooks.co.uk

Rudolf Steiner's Curriculum for Steiner-Waldorf Schools

E. A. Karl Stockmeyer

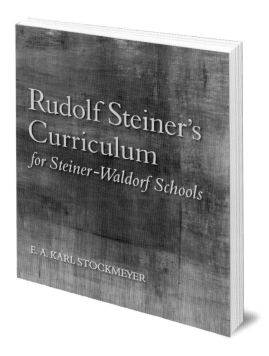

This book is an in-depth exploration of the curriculum of the first Waldorf school, expanding on the original 'Lehrplan'.

Divided into sections, the book outlines Steiner's comments on schools and lessons in general, as well as many details on his thinking on specific issues ranging from different age groups to classroom decoration and arrangement.

This important book for all Steiner-Waldorf teachers gets to the heart of Steiner's ideas on education and child development.

Painting and Drawing in Waldorf Schools

Thomas Wildgruber

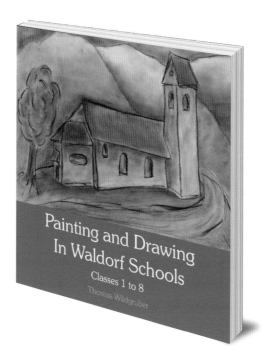

Painting and drawing are key artistic expressions which play an important role in children's physical, emotional and spiritual development.

This comprehensive teachers' manual provides a complete artistic curriculum for Classes One to Eight in Steiner-Waldorf schools (age six to fourteen).

florisbooks.co.uk

A Waldorf Song Book

Brien Masters

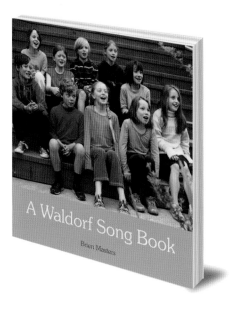

This much-loved book is a collection of over one hundred songs, some well known, some less known, collected over the years by experienced Waldorf teacher Brien Masters.

They are graded for different ages from Class 3 to Class 8 and grouped into festivals and seasons. They include rounds and four-part songs, and musical notation for recorders and other instruments.

This is a wonderful resource for Steiner-Waldorf class teachers, and any teacher or parent looking to introduce music to their classroom or home.

Young gardeners may also enjoy...

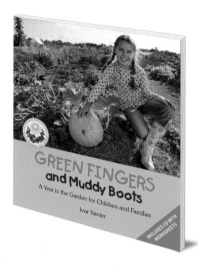

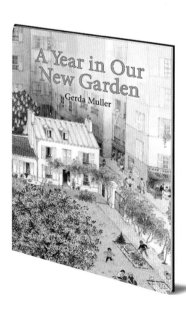